Practical tools, encouraging suggestions, and a warm, loving style make this a real charmer for moms learning how to nurture their offspring.

Barbara Johnson

Spatula Ministries

Carol and Elisa have done it again! Moms who follow the very practical advice in this book will have children who feel deeply loved. Is anything more important?

Rachael Crabb

What every mom needs is her own personal copy of What Every Child Needs. Encouraging. Honest. Practical. Filled with hope and helpful suggestions, this book could well serve as a family life preserver!

Claudia and David Arp

Authors of *10 Great Dates to Energize Your Marriage*

This is a book every mom needs!

Marilyn Meberg

Co-author of *The Joyful Journey*

Elisa and Carol have written a reare gem—a unique combination of celebration of family, passion for developmentally sound parenting, and creative "can-do" encouragement in the fine art of mothering. You will be so glad you're a mom when you read this book!

Valerie Bell

Author of *Getting Out of Your Kids' Faces and Into Their Hearts*

Resources by the Authors

TOGETHER

Children Change a Marriage
Make Room for Daddy
What Every Child Needs Audio Pages®
What Every Child Needs Daybreak®
What Every Mom Needs
What Every Mom Needs Audio Pages®

ELISA MORGAN

Chronicles of Childhood
I'm Tired of Waiting!
Meditations for Mothers
Mom to Mom

CAROL KUYKENDALL

Give Them Wings
Learning to Let Go
A Mother's Footprints of Faith

MOTHERS OF
M♥PS. ...because mothering matters
PRESCHOOLERS

What Every CHILD Needs

MEET YOUR CHILD'S NINE BASIC NEEDS FOR LOVE

Elisa Morgan
Carol Kuykendall

ZONDERVAN

GRAND RAPIDS, MICHIGAN 49530

ZONDERVAN™

What Every Child Needs
Copyright © 1997 by MOPS International, Inc.

Requests for information should be addressed to:

Zondervan, *Grand Rapids, Michigan 49530*

Library of Congress Cataloging-in-Publication Data

Morgan, Elisa, 1955–
  What Every Child Needs : meet your child's nine basic needs for
love / Elisa Morgan and Carol Kuykendall.
    p. cm.
  Includes bibliographical references.
  ISBN: 0-310-23271-6 (softcover)
    1.Mothers. 2. Mother and child. I. Kuykendall, Carol,
  1945– . II. Title.
  HQ759.M862 1997
  649'.1—dc21   97-21801
                           CIP

Published in association with the literary agency of Alive Communications,
Inc., 7680 Goddard Street, Suite 200, Colorado Springs, CO 80920.

Printed in the United States of America

---

01 02 03 04 /❖ DC/ 10 9 8 7 6 5

Mom, what does your child need most?

Me!

My eyes, my ears, my arms, my heart.

Hugs.

Patience.

Acceptance.

To feel important.

A sense of belonging.

A sense of humor.

A mom who knows she has needs too.

Home—a safe haven.

Strings and wings.

Common sense.

Prayer.

Laughter.

Routine.

Firm boundaries.

Flexible edges.

To know Mom and Dad love each other.

Answers (Why is the sky blue? Where do freckles
   come from?)

Freedom to fail.

Love. Love. Love.

Mom, what helps you meet your child's needs?

Counting to ten a lot.

Listening.

Watching.

Being honest about my needs.

Accepting myself.

Using a softer tone of voice.

Being a child with my child.

Going with my instincts.

Tearing up my to-do list.

Being able to forgive. Again and again.

Turning off the TV.

Taking a nap so I'm rested.

Using an answering machine more often.

A microwave.

Using paper plates sometimes.

Noticing when my child does something right.

Letting God love me.

Asking an older mom lots of questions.

Seizing the moment.

Never giving up.

Contents

Acknowledgments

This book represents the efforts of a team of people associated with MOPS International who are dedicated to meeting the needs of mothers of preschoolers. That includes, of course, the need for information and encouragement about the task of raising young children. Specifically, we would like to thank:

Karen Parks, Michele Hall, Mary Beth Lagerborg, and Brenda Quinn, our in-house editors; Gail Burns, our footnotes-finder; Kelly Jacobson, our nimble-fingered processor of words; Lydia Deamer, our cut-and-paste expert; and Cindy Sumner, our Lap Reading expert.

At Zondervan, we'd like to thank:

Sandy VanderZicht and Rachel Boers, our professional editors; and Linda Peterson, our professional laboratory mom and team builder.

We also appreciate Rick Christian for his advocacy.

We're indebted to all the real-life moms who answered our questionnaires. Their comments validate this book.

Finally, we want to thank our children: Eva and Ethan Morgan, and Derek, Lindsay, and Kendall Kuykendall, who have given us a home laboratory to test out our "love language."

Introduction

We all want to be good moms.

We want to give our children what they need when they need it, and we know the early years are important years. But we're often overwhelmed with all the questions and choices. "What does my child need the *most?*" we ask. "What does my child need *right now?*" We're bombarded with advice and opinions. The possibilities often confuse us and rob us of the joy of mothering.

Another question, equally as unsettling, rises to the surface: "What if I know what my child needs, but I'm too tired or too impatient or too busy to meet my child's need at that moment? Then what?" Such an honest question troubles us as we seek to be good moms.

THE "HEART" OF MOTHERING IS LOVE

This book seeks to answer those questions, combining the real-life voices of mothers with the research of experts. MOPS International, an organization founded in 1973 to nurture mothers of preschoolers, asked more than one thousand moms from all over the country: "What does your child need the most?" Not surprisingly, we kept getting variations of the same answer: "My child needs my love." "My child needs me." "My hugs." "My attention." "Unconditional love." "'No matter what' love." "Tough love."

It seemed that the "heart" of mothering is love. Digging a little deeper, however, we found that these mothers recognize their children need different kinds of love at different times. So we identified a child's nine basic needs, using the unique language of love that reflects those needs from a child's perspective, especially during the first years of life.

This book is different from other books about mothering. It's not another one of those "scary mommy" books that makes you worry or feel guilty about all the things you haven't done or can't do. You've seen enough of those. It's not a parenting manual that makes you feel inadequate. It's not a pediatric guide to medical mothering or a child psychologist's book on development.

It is a book written by moms for moms who want to meet their children's most important needs. It slices through all the possible things we could do as mothers and frees us up to do the one thing that matters most: love our children. That's the heart of mothering. It's written to bring confidence that even when we miss doing some things, when we keep our eyes on the heart of mothering, most other things will fall into place.

MOMS HAVE NEEDS TOO!

This book also takes a realistic look at a mother's ability to meet *all* of her children's needs. The truth is, we cannot meet *all* of our children's needs *all* of the time. In an earlier book, *What Every Mom Needs,* we wrote about the nine basic needs of a mother. We said that a mom who recognizes her own needs can become a better mom. In this book we look at the needs of children, but we also look at the ways a mother's needs sometimes bump up against the needs of her child.

Sometimes you are talking on the phone, and you can't give your child the attention she requests. Sometimes you have to be away from home, and you'll miss the opportunity to comfort him when he scrapes his knee. Sometimes your frustration with other problems or your fatigue distracts you from listening well. Sometimes your agendas differ: you want your child to dress a certain way for a certain event, and she wants to choose her own outfit. You need your child to look nice for your friends; your child needs to express her independence. We've all been there. We know about those conflicts of needs.

One woman sent us a prayer in which she expresses this constant conflict as a mother of three.

> *Lord,*
> *When they scribble on the walls, please help me to see a rainbow!*
> *And when I've said something a hundred times, please give me the patience to say it a hundred times more!*
> *And on those particularly annoying days when I tell them to act their age, please help me to remember that they are!*
> *And while we're on the subject of age, Lord, when I begin to lose my temper, please help me to remember to act mine!*
> *And through it all, Lord—the fingerprints and runny noses, messy rooms and unrolled toilet paper, destroyed videotapes and broken knick-knacks—please help me to remember this:*
> *Someday, these will be the days I will long to have back again.*[1]

HOW TO MEET YOUR CHILD'S NEEDS

Mothering matters. But mothers also matter. Therefore, when it comes to recognizing and meeting your child's needs, remember this:

- You can begin to meet your child's needs by recognizing that you, too, have needs.
- You can best meet your child's needs by understanding and accepting your child, but also by understanding and accepting yourself.
- You can best meet your child's needs by realizing that you can't meet all of your child's needs all the time and other people can help.
- You can best meet your child's needs by examining what you liked and didn't like in the way you were mothered.
- You can best meet your child's needs by focusing on the main thing: loving your child. The rest will eventually fall into place.

In the pages that follow, you'll find descriptions of your child's nine core needs, followed by "Love Handles," or suggestions on how to meet these needs starting today. Yes, we all want to be good moms. We hope this book will encourage you and help you understand the important ways you can meet your child's needs by focusing on the heart of mothering.

Getting to the heart of mothering together,

Elisa Morgan and
Carol Kuykendall
for MOPS International

Security:
Hold-Me-Close Love

There. Finally he was down for the night. Sweet-smelling from his bath. Cozy in his cotton sleeper. Tummy full from feeding. Burped. Rocked. And now sound asleep. His lacy lashes touched his cheeks as he lay snug beneath his blanket. A little bump in a big crib.

Janis tiptoed out of the room and down the hall. Six weeks into mothering, she felt like she was getting the hang of her new responsibility. She loved her child beyond words, but sometimes, as she repeated the routines of bathing, feeding, and changing him, she questioned if just anybody could meet these needs for him.

What's so uniquely special about me—his mother? she wondered as she slipped into her own bed and pulled the covers up under her chin. Musing on this question, she soon fell asleep.

Some time later, she awoke with a start to a loud clap of thunder and the sound of rain beating down on the roof. It was pitch-black in the bedroom. Even the night-light in the bathroom was out. Strange. She searched in the darkness for the clock. It, too, was out. Just then a flash of lightning pierced the darkness, followed immediately by a crack of thunder.

Then she heard baby Samuel's cry. She bounded out of bed and rushed down the hall toward his room. His crying

sounded more like a pitiful wail now, a different cry than she'd
ever heard before. In the past few weeks, she'd started to identify his cries: *"I'm hungry. Feed me!!!"* or *"I'm wet. Change
me!!!"* or *"Ouch. Something hurts in my tummy!!!"* But this cry
was new. What did he need?

Opening the door, she realized that his night-light was out
as well. Tree branches scraped the window near his bed, making
eerie sounds in the darkness. Thunder boomed again. She
rushed to the side of his crib and looked down. As her eyes adjusted to the darkness, she saw that his little fists were balled up,
his mouth open, and his feet flailing. He looked so helpless! So
alone! Something touched Janis deep inside. She suddenly knew
exactly what her baby needed. She hadn't read about it in a
book or heard it from her doctor. The response came straight
from her heart.

It's as if his cry said: *"Hold me close, Mommy! Are you there?
I need you! Hold me close!"*

Janis scooped up Samuel's rigid little body, wrapped her
arms around him, and nuzzled him close to her neck. "There,
there, my little one," she said in a reassuring tone as she backed
into the rocking chair. "Mommy's here. Everything's okay. I've
got you now. You're all right." Tenderly she talked to him as
they gently rocked. Gradually Samuel calmed down, his gaze
fixed on her eyes. His tiny fist caught the edge of her nightgown,
and he seemed to respond to her presence—her voice, her smell,
her eyes, the touch of her gown. Soon his little body relaxed. His
breathing became regular, and he closed his eyes again.

As the thunder rumbled outside, Janis continued to rock
her precious baby-boy bundle. Slowly, the understanding came
to her. Her baby's frightened cry in the night had spoken a new
language to her—the language of a baby's need for his mother.
He needs me, she thought. *He needs me uniquely. Not just for
food. Or a clean diaper. Or help with a gas bubble. No. His cry*

tonight communicated a need for security. The message couldn't have been more clear if he had enunciated the words: *"Hold me close, Mommy! I need you!"*

SAFE AND SECURE

As moms, we know that our children have many needs. The question of how we can ever learn to meet them all plagues us. We want so much to be good moms and to take care of our children's needs. But how and where do we begin? Sometimes we feel overwhelmed and confused by the enormity of the task.

Perhaps the starting place is with the most basic of all needs: the need for security—to feel loved and safe and protected. A child needs security to develop. On this basis he slowly builds his ability to cope in the world: to trust, to learn, to experience a sense of confidence and well-being, and to develop loving, lasting relationships with other people. Without a sense of security, a child may exist, but he will not grow to be all that he can be. A mother's nurturing love, which provides for her child's security, is one of her first and greatest contributions to his whole life.

But what does this love look like? How does a child express the need for this love, and how does a mother meet that need?

Quite simply, the need for security is a need for a Hold-Me-Close Love, expressed by the child in messages like: "I need you to hold me close when I feel afraid. Or when I have an owie. Or when my tummy hurts. Sometimes I just need to know that you are near so you can hold me close and help me feel safe."

This kind of love is described as the bond between mother and child.

When we were on a trip, my two-year-old fell asleep without her usual bedtime routine. She woke up about 5:00 A.M. shouting, "My prayers! I need to say my prayers!" She would not be quieted until a groggy mom prayed with her.

— ❧ —

THE BOND DEFINED

We hear lots about the importance of maternal bonding. We have pictures in our minds of what it looks like. The newborn baby is placed on the mother's tummy immediately after delivery, and, for one incredible moment, they make eye contact. Instinctively, the mother begins to tenderly caress her child. Later, the mother carries her baby around in a cloth sling or front pack, so the child is snuggled close to her heart as she goes about her work. The mother rocks her baby and speaks in soothing tones, developing a unique body-and-soul love language with her child.

This bond between mother and child is one of the most basic and important ingredients in a baby's development. It is mother love. Connection. Attachment. Whatever you call it, this bond is the basis of security in every individual. Infant researcher Stanley Greenspan identifies it as an "essential partnership." Psychologist Urie Bronfenbrenner defines a bond as "a strong, mutual, irrational, emotional attachment (with someone) who is committed to the child's well-being and development, preferably for life."[1] It is a deep, unchangeable confidence of permanent connection. A "young child's hunger for his mother's love and presence is as great as his hunger for food," writes John Bowlby in his book *Attachment*.[2]

Notice several key terms in these descriptions. First, this bond is *mutual*. It is a two-way connection. The baby must bond with the mother. The baby must become convinced that she is *present* and that she can be trusted to meet his most basic needs. And the mother must bond with the baby. She must become convinced that she is uniquely needed in her child's life and that she alone best meets certain needs. Meeting her baby's needs can touch and satisfy deep places of longing within her.

The bond is also *irrational*. It is illogical and absurd. The mother looks at her red, wrinkled, raisin-like newborn and exclaims, "Isn't she beautiful!" Undoubtedly, she is rational, but she is bonding!

The bond is *child-focused*. It centers primarily on the well-being of the child. A mother sacrifices to meet the needs of the child, even when it isn't convenient or valued by others. A mother loses sleep to soothe a fretful baby or changes a schedule to be available for a child who needs her.

The bond is also *permanent*. The mother is committed to the child for life. And the child to the mother. Day in and day out. Being there. Meeting needs. Teaching one another that relationships that persevere are relationships that last.

Most important, the bond is *foundational to the child's future*. For decades, child experts have agreed that this mother-child bond is the basis upon which everything else in life is built.

- *Physically.* A baby's brain is a jumble of trillions of neurons, a work in progress, waiting to be wired into a mind. *Newsweek* magazine reported that the experiences of early childhood, specifically the basic bond of mother and child, help form the brain's circuits for music, math, language, and emotions. All learning and feelings are built upon the foundation of this bond.[3]

- *Socially.* John Bowlby, who studied the attachment of babies and mothers, said that babies need a "secure base" from which to venture out to explore their world. From this base, a baby develops a sense of his own worthiness, conscience, and the capacity for intimacy in later significant relationships.[4]

  In 1940, Sigmund Freud wrote that a baby's relationship with her mother is "unique, without parallel, established unalterably for a whole lifetime as the first and strongest love object and as the prototype of all later love relationships for both sexes."[5]

- *Emotionally.* In their book *The Mom Factor,* Drs. Henry Cloud and John Townsend attribute many of the components that make up our "emotional IQ" to our bond with our mother. "Not only do we learn our patterns of intimacy, relating, and separateness from Mother, but we also learn about how to handle failure, troublesome emotions, expectations and ideals, grief and loss . . ."[6]

Dr. Brenda Hunter, an expert on attachment issues, stresses that early bonding with the mother affects later success in all endeavors: Mother "remains bound to us by an invisible tether as we mature. If the relationship is close, we remember those feelings of warmth and security we had as children while we are making our own mark on the world."[7]

NO ONE BUT MOM

While children can find Hold-Me-Close Love in patches and spots in other relationships, the bond with their mother is the most unique and vital source of security for their lives. No one can meet this need in our children like we can! In their book, *Mother in the Middle,* authors Deborah Shaw Lewis and Charmaine Crouse Yoest list the special ways that a child responds to the mother in the bonding process.

- Newborn babies prefer a higher-pitched voice. Not only are most mothers' voices naturally higher than that of a father, but mothers instinctively talk to a newborn in "mother-ese," a voice pitched higher than their usual voices.
- A newborn baby moves in rhythm to his mother's voice, enticing his mother to talk to him more.

- Infants recognize, attend to, and are comforted by their mothers' voices within the first week. Mothers report being able to distinguish their babies' cries from those of other babies while still in the hospital.
- Babies prefer being rocked head to toe—as in a mother's arms—rather than the back-and-forth rocking of a baby swing.
- By the time a baby is five days old, he recognizes and prefers the smell of his own mother's milk.
- Mother's milk provides specific immunities for her child against the germs in their particular environment.
- By the time a baby is three to four weeks old, an observer can look at the baby's face, not knowing with whom she is playing, and successfully tell who is interacting with the baby: mother, father, or stranger. With a mother, the baby's movements and facial expressions are smooth and rhythmic, anticipating a calm, low-key interaction. With a father, the baby tenses up, her face lights up, and movements become agitated, in anticipation of father play.[8]

Author Katherine Butler Hathaway aptly describes the uniqueness and completeness of the mother-child bond in her writings, *The Journal and Letters of the Little Locksmith*. "She is their food and their bed and their extra blanket when it grows cold in the night; she is their warmth and health and their shelter; she is the one they want to be near when they cry. She is the only person in the whole world or in a whole lifetime, who can be these things to her children. Somehow even her clothes feel different to her children's hands

On a recent really hectic day, my four-year-old told his grandmother, "All I'd like to do is get back into mommy's tummy and have some peace and quiet."

— ❧ —

from anybody else's clothes. Only to touch her skirt or her sleeve makes a troubled child feel better."[9]

CAN I REALLY MEET THIS NEED IN MY CHILD?

While there's much research to support the importance of the mother uniquely meeting the child's need for Hold-Me-Close Love, more than a few moms find themselves strangling on some of the following personal doubts.

"There's Not Enough of Me for My Child."

We're tired. We never have a second to ourselves. And there goes the baby's colicky cries again. All we do is give, give, give, until there is nothing left. Sometimes we just want to let that sweet child cry. Or let someone else step in.

Not one of us is enough—by ourself—to meet our child's entire need for Hold-Me-Close Love. We are not machines, nor are we divine. We will lose our patience. We will sleep through a midnight alarm-cry for food. We will be away from our child when she wants us and only us. But we can meet this need *most* of the time. And that's what matters. If we take care of ourselves, making sure we eat right and try to get normal amounts of sleep and a break now and then, we'll have enough to meet our child's need for security.

"My Child's Neediness Scares Me."

The need for security runs deep. And because it is one of the first needs evidenced, it usually catches us unprepared. Somehow, when our child expresses this need for Hold-Me-Close Love, she hooks into a spot deep within our hearts and touches our own need for security. If *we* weren't held, listened to, or kept safe, we're bound to struggle with responding just right to providing security for our child.

Some moms find that the years of first becoming a mom are good times for reevaluating their relationships with their parents and for reexamining what they want to repeat and what they want to change in their own mothering. It's important to be gentle with yourself here. These needs are core, and they do make a difference for the future of your child. But your child is also resilient and will grow as you commit to growing too.

COMPONENTS OF SECURITY

The need for security is really a need for three major components in a child's life. Let's look at them one at a time.

Safety

To prosper, every child needs to know that he is safe. Physical safety is found in shelter, cleanliness, health, food, and protection from harm. Emotional safety comes from appropriate boundaries, expectations, and helpful interpretations by adults in the child's world. Drs. Henry Cloud and John Townsend express this overall need for safety in their book *The Mom Factor.*

> As little people, we experience the world as dangerous. We feel alone. We don't have love inside—we have overwhelming needs and feelings. This is painful, and you can see this pain on the face of any infant who wants to be picked up or of the child who is terrified of something in her imagination. *The child does not have safety inside, but danger. Safety can only be found in the mother or in whoever is providing the mothering.* Safety comes in the form of a person who is predictable, stable, and danger-free.... With-

My three-year-old son fell off the swing set and later said, "I knew you would come and save me."

— ❧ —

out this person, the child remains in a state of panic or anxiety, unable to love or learn.[10]

Unconditional Love

The second component of security is unconditional love. We like to call it "no matter what" love. This love convinces a child that "no matter what" she does, thinks, or is, she will be loved. Family expert Ron Hutchcraft describes it from a child's point of view: "Children find out where they really stand when they embarrass their parents or rebel against their beliefs. Sometimes they seem to be asking, 'Can you love me like this?' 'Can you love me defiant?' 'Can you love me when I've broken your heart?' If you can find the grace to say yes, you have given the highest love there is—unconditional love."

He goes on to say that "ironically, *when your children are the least lovable, they need your love the most*. When you feel the least like loving them, they will be able to feel your love the most."[11]

Trust

Another component is trust. We *trust* another when we are able to invest in a relationship with that person. Trust is the basis for all good and growing relationships. If a child learns to trust his

When my daughter was seven months old, I was rocking her. Her head was on my shoulder and she was cooing. Then she bit me, hard. My first reaction was to yell, "Hey!" This scared her and she trembled and cried. I tried to calm her. She finally calmed down with her head on my shoulder and I was saying, "It's okay," when she bit me again, in the neck and harder this time. I held her out and yelled, "Hey, didn't you learn anything?!" Her eyes filled with crocodile tears. As I held her, I realized that she was doubting if I loved her. I think that made me realize that it's not what I say or how I am when she is good, but how I react when she makes mistakes that makes her feel unconditionally loved.

— ❧ —

mother, he will be able to transfer the experience of trust by risking trust in others. If not, psychologist William Damon believes that "there is little hope that an infant can feel the confidence in the self necessary to establish individuality and autonomy."[12] A child builds trust as he learns he can count on his mother.

SECURITY RISKS

What happens when a child's need for security is not met? The answer is simple, born out by the results of many studies on children who are deprived of this kind of Hold-Me-Close Love. This child is at risk. Without the security of a consistent mother-child bond, the child suffers.

Experts define various disorders related to this lack of bonding. The most commonly known is the "failure to thrive" syndrome, where babies given only rudimentary feedings and changings and deprived of loving nurturance fail to gain weight and sometimes withdraw from their surroundings. Where no physical causes can be determined for this condition, it is concluded that the baby experiences a sense of parental rejection. Another is known as "attachment disorder" seen in institutionalized children who spent their first years without the love or nurturing that newborns normally receive. Children with this disorder frequently have physical, developmental, and psychological problems.

A lack of bonding also causes emotional damage. Valerie Bell, in her book *Getting Out of Your Kids Faces and Into Their Hearts,* claims that an insecure child begins to believe that she is unlovable, which disturbs the development of her character. Here are some symptoms that are apt to be displayed by character-disturbed children:

1. Lack of ability to give and receive affection
2. Self-destructive behavior

   3. Cruelty to others or to pets
   4. Phoniness
   5. Stealing, hoarding, and gorging
   6. Lack of long-term childhood friends
   7. Extreme control problems
   8. Speech pathology
   9. Abnormalities in eye contact
   10. The parents seem unreasonably angry
   11. Preoccupation with blood, fire, and gore
   12. Superficial attractiveness and friendliness with strangers
   13. Learning disorders
   14. Crazy lying[13]

   Don't confuse these more serious behaviors with a child's
normal expression of fears, such as separation anxiety or middle-
of-the-night fears or the fear of abandonment, that a parent may
die or go away. Many children experience these fears at different levels and different stages of development. Usually they are
temporary and require a mother's sensitive and soothing response, a combination of Hold-Me-Close Love and gentle
words of assurance.

   According to Drs. Cloud and Townsend, "a mother contains a child's scary feelings. A child feels alone with his feelings
and feels that they are 'bigger' than him. When mother takes
him up and rocks him, she 'takes in' her child's scary feelings.
The child has a place to put them, with someone who isn't
afraid of them. *She exchanges these feelings for calmness, repose,
and love.* It's as if the child dumped some toxic wastes into mom
and received good food in return."[14]

   Whew! From all these experts and information emerges a
strong, unavoidable fact: babies need their mothers to provide
a secure base for their futures. When security is built from birth
in a bonded mother-child relationship, a child is given the tools

necessary to accomplish the single most important challenge of his life: growing up. The goal of childhood is independence, and independence is achieved only as that child goes through an appropriate period of dependence, most ideally on his mother.

HANDING OUT HOLD-ME-CLOSE LOVE

Okay. So you're convinced. Our children need security and, as mothers, we have a unique opportunity to meet this vital need. So how do we do it? We don't look backwards and spend a lot of time wishing we'd done things differently in our children's lives. We simply start from where we are right now by including each of the following in their lives.

Security Through Protection

From childproofing your home to feeding your baby a balanced diet to scheduling regular doctor checkups to the careful selection of caretakers, a sense of security begins with physically protecting our children. We show our love by exercising basic safety precautions. We continue to meet this need as they grow up by using recommended car seats, buckling up seat belts, providing bike helmets, and teaching safety about crossing streets and dealing with strangers, animals, and swimming pools, to name just a few. In many cases, accidents or crises occur because of ignorance. If you don't know what your child needs in order to be safe, ask an older mom, your pediatrician, or another expert.

Security Through Touch

Most moms know that touching is a powerful way to communicate love to a child. Picking up a crying child to soothe him communicates that he is loved. Dr. Frederic Burke, a pediatrician in Washington, D.C., says, "I firmly believe that early physical experience with parents' loving hands and arms is imprinted in the child's mind; and while apparently forgotten, it has a tremendous influence on the child's ego and the kind of adolescent he or she becomes."[15]

In his book *If I Could Raise My Kids Again*, William Coleman confesses that he would do things differently if given a second chance with his kids. "My goal would be to show more affection to my children, to receive more from them." Further, he believes that the "best place for a child to be nurtured is at the knee or on the lap of an adult who hugs, kisses, smiles, and speaks words of tender encouragement. Children who miss this experience often spend decades looking for the real thing."[16]

Sometimes when my child is cranky I hug him, because that squeezes out all the "growly bugs" inside him.

— ❧ —

My three-year-old son had hurt his hand twice in the same day and wanted me to cuddle him. I was trying to make supper. I asked him, "Which do you want, supper or cuddles?" He wanted cuddles. At that moment his soul needed food more than his body.

— ❧ —

Researchers at the University of Miami Medical School's Touch Research Institute showed that premature babies who received three fifteen-minute periods of slow, firm massage strokes each day showed forty-seven percent greater weight gain than children who didn't receive this attention. The study also revealed improved sleep, alertness, and activity and eight months later, greater mental and physical skills.[17]

Older children respond just as hungrily. In his book *The Key to Your Child's Heart,* Gary Smalley talks of a family handhold "where we interlock our little fingers. Every member of our family knows that this is our secret family tradition hold. . . . and it is a personal, physical sign of affection. . . . A real sense of meaningfulness and security comes from touching."[18]

Infant massage. Cuddle communication. Soothing hugs. Hand-holding over a mealtime prayer. Smooches under chins and on chubby tummies. When you include touch in your security measures, you can see your children grow.

Security Through Eye Contact

From the moment a newborn baby opens his eyes, he is searching his blurry world to find the eyes of another human being. The baby is trying to communicate with that eye-to-eye contact. His question is, "Can I trust you? Is this world going to be a safe place for me? Am I going to be accepted and loved?" Amazingly, God designed mothers to meet this need, because it's been said that the space between the mother's face and the crook of an arm where a baby is held is exactly the amount of space needed for a baby to focus on the eyes and face of a mother.

Dr. Ross Campbell, child development expert, believes that "eye contact is one of the main sources of a child's emotional nurturing."[19] As such, he urges parents to avoid using it negatively (like in those rolled eyes that communicate "I told you so" or glares meant to wither a child with the message, "You'd better not do that!").

Take advantage of the power of good eye contact. Look straight into your child's eyes; couple that message with words of praise, and you are meeting your child's need for security. Even care-filled discipline, given in love with eyeball-to-eyeball tenderness, can build security in your child.

Security Through Presence

Over and over again, child development research shows us that the most important years in the development of human personality are from birth to three years of age. Naturally, if a mother wants to influence that development, she must be physically present. Much of that time seems insignificant, as if nothing is happening, yet the child needs the reassurance that her mother is near. That reassurance is what gives her the confidence to take baby steps away at her own rate of stepping.

"Mommy, watch me!" "Look Mommy!" "Come outside with me." These are my child's expressions of a need for my presence.

— ❧ —

The child often expresses that need in a setting like this: You're in the kitchen making dinner and your toddler is building with blocks in the next room.

"Mama?" she asks.

"What?" you answer.

"Mama?" she asks again.

"What?"

"Mama?" she repeats.

"I'm right here, honey, what do you want?" you reply, a bit frustrated.

The greatest indicator to me that my children's needs are not being met is when their fighting, whining, and crying increases tenfold. When I increase my attention to them, they respond with better behavior.

— ❧ —

"Nothing. I just wanted to know you are there."

A child often uses a security object like a "blankie" or favorite toy to minimize the stress of separation anxiety, especially as that child begins to grow up and venture outside the mother's presence to a friend's house, daycare, or preschool.

Often moms worry that their children will carry these raggedy old security blankets with them all the way through elementary school, but have you ever seen a high school senior walking across the platform to get a diploma with a "blankie" in hand? Child development expert Dr. Mary Manz Simon claims that "separation from a security object usually follows a pattern: the child needs it everywhere, the child needs it at specific times or places, the child starts to 'forget' he needs it, and the child doesn't miss it or realizes he doesn't need it."[20]

Our children gain a sense of security through our presence and, as mothers, we make an intentional choice to be present for them. As Ruth Bell Graham, mother of five, concluded, "If I cannot give my children a perfect mother, I can at least give them more of the one they've got—and make that one more loving. I will be available. I will take time to listen, time to play . . . time to counsel and encourage."[21]

Security Through Consistency

Security comes with predictability, and predictability comes through consistency. Consistency means making a plan (or rules) and not changing that plan all the time. A child needs predictability in life. When he knows that a certain action will always elicit a certain response, he grows confident that he can interact with his world in a meaningful way. And when a mother works to communicate a given message in a consistent manner, she meets her child's needs, and her communication gets through to the child she wants to influence.

Consistency includes consistent love and attention and discipline and routines. Children thrive on consistent routines. Breakfast, then brush your teeth, then get dressed, then make your bed, then play. Later in

When our six-year-old came to us as a foster child, he was so surprised to have us sit together as a family each night. After our first meal together, he asked me, "Do we do this every day?" To his delight I responded, "Yes." He thrived on dependable routines.

— ❧ —

the day it is wash your hands, eat your dinner, take your bath, brush your teeth, read a few stories, say your prayers, and go to bed. Such count-on-it, predictable routines layer security into the everyday life of a child.

A child also needs the consistent demonstration of love lived out in the home. Not only love for them, but love for the other members of a family, especially a spouse. As the old saying goes, "The best thing I can do for my kids' security is to let them know I love their daddy." In a two-parent home, kids feel more secure when they see that Mommy and Daddy love each other.

GETTING TO THE HEART
OF HOLD-ME-CLOSE LOVE

Building security into your child today makes sense for tomorrow. Children who can trust their parents to anticipate their needs today become secure, well-behaved children. As Valerie Bell says, "A secure child is less apt to act out or develop behavior problems. Between the nurturing parent and the well-cared-for child is an exquisite bond that is a beauty to behold—and even more beautiful to experience."[22]

The four of us were snuggling on the loveseat and my older two children said at the same time, "I love doing this, it makes me feel so warm and fuzzy."

— ❧ —

"I need Hold-Me-Close Love," our children tell us with their cries, their eyes, their actions, and their hearts. They have a foundational need for security, to feel loved and safe—and when we recognize that need and invest ourselves in meeting it, we are investing ourselves in their futures.

Love Handles

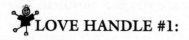 **LOVE HANDLE #1:**

Safety

Safety at home

Minimize the risk of accidents by childproofing your homes. (This list is not exhaustive. Be sure to include your own common sense rules for providing safety in your home.)

- Keep babies away from the cooking area in the kitchen. Keep all sharp objects and hot foods away from counter edges. Turn pan handles toward the back of the stove.
- Put child-resistant latches on all lower drawers and cupboards. Move cleaning solutions and other toxic products to a higher shelf.
- Place special covers over unused electrical wallsockets.
- Put corner protectors on sharp edges.
- Place bouncy chairs, swings, and bassinets on the floor. Keep them away from open doors, fires, or tabletops.
- Keep table lamps, telephones, and all cords out of reach.
- Install gates at the bottom and top of stairs, and across the kitchen door.
- Use a baby monitor.
- Never leave a baby alone in a bathtub. Always check the bathwater temperature before putting the child in the tub. Use a nonskid mat on the bottom of the tub.
- Always put a car seat in the backseat of a car.
- Put a baby to sleep on his back, not his tummy.

Safety away from home—
Choosing a day care provider or baby-sitter

What children need most in a baby-sitter or day care provider is the assurance that they are safe and nurtured. The place has to be physically safe, emotionally secure, and developmentally appropriate. Here are some guidelines to look for:

- A shared set of common values, about TV watching and discipline, for instance. Ask specific questions to get these answers.

- Commitment to safety. Again, ask questions. If the care is provided in another home, look for safety hazards. Is the primary focus your child, or are there too many other distractions? Is the provider easily distracted? What does she consider to be age-appropriate activities, and what is the mix of ages and number of other children also cared for by the same provider?

- Communication skills. Is this person willing to openly share what is going on with the children in her care? Will she identify and share any unusual behaviors? Does she welcome your questions or get defensive?[23]

- Provide a "baby-sitter's information sheet." If you have a computer, you can make up your own form and fill in the appropriate information each time you leave your child with a new caretaker. The sheet should include your child's name and nickname; your full name; where you can be reached; when you will return; your pediatrician's phone number; the phone number of a neighbor or other contact person; what your child can or cannot eat; any allergies your child may have; any medicine your child needs to take; a signed statement giving the baby-sitter permission to seek emergency care for your child; and any routines that need to be followed while you are gone. Add any others important to the care of your child.

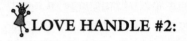 **LOVE HANDLE #2:**

Touch

Cuddle time and feeding

Babies hunger for our touch, almost as much as for food. So we combine the two by holding and cuddling them while feeding them. So often, busy moms are tempted to prop up the bottle or prop up her baby at her breast, so the hands are free to do other things, but experts tell us that feeding time is an important time to pass on the nourishment of not only food, but also love, given through touching and holding the baby. So get a rocking chair—and start some "cuddle communication" with your child.

Age-appropriate touching

As children grow, some resist the same kinds of hugs and kisses they received as babies, but all children, regardless of age, need appropriate physical contact. Ruffle your son's hair, give him back rubs, or play the "thumb war game," which requires hand-holding. Put your arm around your daughter instead of taking her hand as you walk across a busy parking lot. Hold hands as a family while saying grace before a meal. Offer to give a foot massage. Tuck your child into bed and sit down on the bed to talk.

Tender hygiene

Any care of the body can be done with a nurturing touch. Instead of using a hair dryer, towel dry your child's hair, using it as an opportunity to give a gentle head massage. Think about the ways you touch your children while you are washing, combing, brushing, or manicuring them. All these functions offer opportunities to give a child a gentle, loving touch.

Hand signals—A touching language of love

Many mothers invent their own special language of hand-touching with a young child and use this tender form of communication in church, in a meeting, at a library, or anywhere touching is more appropriate than words. Some examples of this language include: One squeeze means, "Do you love me?" Three squeezes is the answer, "I love you." Running your finger over the tops and bottoms of your child's fingers (like peaks and valleys) means, "I love you higher than the mountaintops and deeper than the oceans." Even a gentle hand massage communicates a message. Together, make up your own touching language of love.

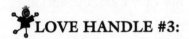 **LOVE HANDLE #3:**

Eye contact

- Play peek-a-boo.
- Look at your child when speaking to or listening to him.
- Get down on her level by getting on your knees more often, so you can see eye-to-eye.
- Take a child into your lap whenever you can.
- When he says, "Watch me!", stop and watch him. Clap. Acknowledge that you have watched.

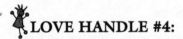 **LOVE HANDLE #4:**

Presence

Recognize the priority of your presence in your child's life

This poem entitled, "Babies Don't Keep," may help.

Cleaning and scrubbing
Can wait 'til tomorrow,
For babies grow up
We've learned to our sorrow.
So quiet down cobwebs . . .
Dust go to sleep.
I'm rocking my baby
And babies don't keep.

Author unknown

Five golden moments in a child's day

These are the quality moments when your presence counts most:

1. The Wake-up: It is important for a child to have some parent-love in the first conscious moment of her day.
2. The Sendoff: Horses, Olympians, and children run a good race when they get off to a good start. As often as possible, you should be there for breakfast and your child's departure to school.
3. The Reception: If you want to get a real reading on how the "game" went, you have to be there when the "player" comes off the field. Your presence when your child comes in the door says "I love you." Your responsibility at the "reception" is mostly to hug, to listen without judgment, to notice your child is home, and to just be available.
4. The Debriefing: This may come right after The Reception. Kids need to debrief their day—not to be interrogated but to report, celebrate, evaluate, or explode. Again, your role is to listen. Your undivided attention communicates that you care.
5. The Happy Ending: If "all's well that ends well," it's good for a parent to be there at the end of the day. It's

a time for "I love you," an "I'm sorry," or a "thank you." It puts a period on the end of the day.[24]

Your presence in your absence

If you are employed outside the home or have to be gone overnight:

- Take your child to your workplace so she can see where you are when you're away.
- Give your child a picture of yourself to carry in his pocket with the message, "I'm always thinking about you, and I'm always close to you."
- Read a favorite story and tape it so your child can listen to you reading it, over and over again.
- Ask for something to remember your child by when you are going away, such as a rock from a rock collection or a little note or drawing.
- Call at an agreed-upon time to say good morning or good night.

Lullabies

The soft sound of a mother's voice soothes a child and brings a reassuring sense of security. You don't have to be a recording artist to have exactly the right sound your child needs. So just hum a lullaby, or get a tape of lullabies and sing along.

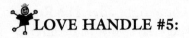LOVE HANDLE #5:

Trust

Says William Coleman in *If I Could Raise My Kids Again*, "To teach my children more about trust, I'd:

- let them jump off more kitchen counters into my waiting arms.

- hold them upside down in the living room and hear them laugh.
- encourage them to free-fall backward into my waiting arms.
- tell them I'd be by to pick them up at three o'clock and then be there on time.
- promise them ice cream for dessert and show up with a cold sack in my arms.
- tell them I'm taking them fishing and then keep my word."[25]

MOM READING:

5 Needs Your Child Must Have Met at Home, Ron Hutchcraft
If I Could Raise My Kids Again, William Coleman
The Mom Factor, Henry Cloud and John Townsend
Mother in the Middle, Deborah Shaw Lewis and Charmaine Crouse Yoest
Seven Things Children Need, John Drescher
What Every Mom Needs, Elisa Morgan and Carol Kuykendall
What Every Mother Needs to Know, Brenda Hunter

LAP READING:

Goodnight Moon, Margaret Wise Brown
Love You Forever, Robert Munsch
Pat the Bunny, Dorothy Kunhardt
Runaway Bunny, Margaret Wise Brown
When You Were a Baby, Deborah Shaw Lewis and Gregg Lewis

Two

Affirmation:
Crazy-About-Me Love

I'm going home!"

The announcement came from two houses down, where four-year-old Madeline was playing on the sidewalk with her neighborhood buddies. Sharon, sitting on her front steps, looked up from her magazine and watched as her daughter stomped up the street toward her. She soon plopped down on the step next to her, folded her chubby little arms across her chest, and stuck out her bottom lip, the way she did when she was determined not to cry.

"They don't like me," she told her mother. "They won't let me play with them." With those words, her tears came, streaking dirt down her cherub cheeks.

"Tell me what happened, Pumpkin," Sharon prompted as she wrapped her arm around her toddler.

Madeline gulp-sobbed her way through an explanation. "Jacob wouldn't let me carry his flashlight! He said I was too little and I might break it! He's so mean, Mommy! I'm *not* too little!" Exhausted from this outburst, she collapsed into the hollow of her mother's arm.

Sharon stroked her child's hair. It was so painful to see her daughter rejected and misunderstood like this. Another reminder that as a mom, she couldn't prevent the wounds her child would experience in the world. But maybe she could soften their impact with love and encouragement.

Scooping Madeline up into her lap, Sharon gently brushed her daughter's hair away from her sticky cheeks and kissed her forehead. Then she perched her daughter on her knees, held her hands, and looked straight into her wide, sad eyes, eyeball-to-eyeball.

"Madeline, do you know how wonderful you are?" she asked.

Madeline shook her head and pulled a hand free to wipe her eyes.

"Madeline, you are the most wonderful-est girl in the whole wide world! I love your button nose." Sharon smooched it quickly. "I love your cherry-red cheeks." She pecked them and continued. "I love your eyelashes and your adorable little eary ears." She bestowed tiny kisses on her daughter's eyes and ears. "I love you from the top of your head all the way down to your twinkly little toes." She bent Madeline's head forward for a kiss and then picked up her sandaled feet and smooched her dimpled toes. "I love your heart," pointing at her chest, "your kindness, your fun ideas, your sweet little sharing spirit."

Madeline stopped crying and watched her mother, wide-eyed. She hung on to every word, giggled through the kisses, and eagerly followed from one affirmation to the next. Hungry from her very soul for these endearments, she opened, like a baby bird, to receive her mother's nurture.

Finally Sharon hugged her daughter close to her chest. "Oh, Madeline," she exclaimed, " I'm absolutely crazy about you!"

MIRRORED LOVE

All children need affirmation. They need to know and believe and feel that they are *utterly* loveable, and they need to be reminded of that message again and again and again! Their hearts and souls are hungry to know that someone has Crazy-About-Me Love for them. Such knowledge becomes the very foundation of their self-image and understanding. And from that foundation comes a joyful confidence for future achievements and relationships. As Victor Hugo wrote, "The supreme happiness of life is the conviction that we are loved."

Young children develop an understanding of who they are and how they are loved by absorbing descriptions of themselves from others. It is not an intellectual experience, but a feeling experience that comes from being in a relation-

My son and I had the tradition of a morning hug (big one) and morning kiss (noisier the better) upon arising. One morning when my son got up, I was distracted. He followed me around. When I finally focused on his presence, he tapped his chest, as if to say, "Here I am. Notice me."

— ❧ —

ship with another person, a mother especially. Drs. Henry Cloud and John Townsend say that "you may know intellectually that you are loved, but if you never felt loved . . . your feelings won't match up with what you know intellectually."[1]

A child's self-image comes not from performance, but from relationships and from the way they believe other people perceive them. They form their self-esteem by evaluating how other significant people view them. Later in life, they are able to love others to the degree that they experienced their own loveableness. As Dr. Ross Campbell puts it, "As the moon reflects the sun, children basically reflect love, but they do not initiate love. If love is given to them, they return it. If none is given, they have none to return."[2]

Who can better meet this need than Mom? Moms are the ones who live in the day-to-day world of their children, observing victory and defeat, acceptance and rejection, contentment and frustration. Moms are the ones who have a unique opportunity to influence their children by reflecting their preciousness. As mothers, we are our children's first mirror, reflecting back to them their worth. No wonder they stare deeply into each reflection we offer, taking it into their very souls!

Several aspects bear remembering as we mirror our child's value through affirmation.

A Steady Reflection

The affirmation we offer our children is most effective if it is consistent. Our children need to know we're crazy about them both when they're wonderful and we truly feel it and when they mess up and we don't feel it at all. That means reflecting our love for them when we're taken in by their doll-baby darlingness and can hardly hold ourselves back, as well as when we're frustrated with their wetting their beds or spilling their milk. In every moment, good and bad, our children need to know they are loveable.

When you've just found on the wallpaper a new mural in black permanent marker, you need some time and distance from the offending artist. But that child needs the reaffirmation of your love.

— ❧ —

I play a game with my preschoolers. They ask, "Would you love me if . . ." Usually we start by focusing on looks: "Would you love me if I had three eyes and my nose on my tummy?" Gradually we move on to things like, "Would you love me if I broke your favorite plate?"

— ❧ —

Mirrored Messages

Meeting the need for affirmation means mirroring specific messages to our children such as:

1. *I'll always love you!* Nothing you can ever do or say or even think will change my love for you. When you do something bad, like tell a lie, I won't like what you *do*, but I'll always love you.

2. *I believe in you!* I know you, and I believe that you are growing and becoming all that you can be. When I see you sharing your book with your little sister, I see you are growing into a kind person. When I see you struggle to pull your sheets up to make your bed, I see that in your heart you want to do a good job, and I know you can do it!

3. *I'm on your side!* No matter what happens or what you feel, I'm on your side. When a friend makes fun of you or is just plain mean, you can know that I will always stand up for you!

4. *I'm your greatest fan!* When others look away or hurt your feelings, I will continue to cheer for you. I'm on your side. I'm crazy about you! I want to hear your words, see your discoveries, and enjoy your creative mind because all these things make you who you are.

When a child receives these messages consistently and knows they are from the heart, he develops confidence that he is indeed loveable and therefore can risk loving others.

When We, as Moms, Warp the Reflection . . .

As much as we yearn to offer these positive messages to our children, we sometimes find ourselves actually warping the very message we want to give. Or our needs and their needs conflict.

"I don't know how to offer affirmation."

Perhaps you came from a family where compliments were few and where criticism and sarcasm were rampant. It may be difficult for you to wrap your tongue around affirmation and drag it from your lips. Start simple, with the physical attributes or actions of your child. Start small, with one compliment each day. Just start. Even though you may have been under-affirmed, you can learn to lavish praise on your children.

"I'm not really crazy about my child."

It's not unusual to feel less than thrilled about some aspect of your child. Perhaps she is a girl and you wanted a boy. Maybe he is bookish and you are boisterous. It may be that she continually spits up and has to be changed a million times a day—and so do you. Or it could be that your child is less than what you wanted in some other way: not athletic, not pretty, not interested in what interests you.

Unconditional love is the hardest for me—a firstborn perfectionist. I have a hard time conveying love for the child when the behavior isn't what I want it to be. As a child I was given "conditional" love and I truly desire to break that cycle.

— ❧ —

Such an admission is painful for us as moms. But it is an important admission nonetheless. As adults, we know that we do not encourage our children by constantly hinting at what we wish they were.

You can get past this bump by facing squarely who your child is and determining to help him or her be the very best at whatever he or she is. Grieve if you need to. Then let go of your predetermined expectations and take up the challenge of meeting the needs of your child through affirming. What *do* you love about your little one? Tell her. What *are* you crazy about? Focus on this, and you will be surprised at how much more you discover you adore in addition.

AFFIRMATION . . . AGAIN AND AGAIN AND AGAIN!

Repetition and variety are critical in offering affirmation. Children need Crazy-About-Me Love again and again and again and in lots of different ways! A child's hunger and need for the soul-food of affirmation is much like physical hunger. One recipe works fine for certain stages of life but, as children grow and change, they develop tastes and needs for a greater variety of foods. And one feeding only lasts so long before a child's heart starts growling for more nourishing affirmation. A new day brings a new need.

I ask my daughter, "What do you have?"
She says, "Determination!"
Then I ask if that's good.
She says, "Yes, I stick to it like peanut butter."
With my son, I ask, "Why do I call you 'Sunshine'?"
He says, "Cuz I bring you so much joy!"
In our conversations, I try to remind them of their good characteristics.

— ❧ —

Fortunately, we can say "I'm crazy about you!" in many ways. Some methods will be easy for you. They'll fit your personality and flow from your heart. Others will be new to you, and you'll need to practice them. Still others may never quite fit for you and your child. Find the styles that work for you and serve them up regularly, giving your child a steady diet of affirmation.

Time and Attention

"Mom, watch this!"

"Mommy, can you play with me?"

"Mommy, read me this book!"

"Mom, I can't do this. Will you help?"

"Mom, will you take me to the store?"

"Mom . . . Mom . . . Mom . . . ?"

The requests keep coming. Starting with unintelligible midnight wails, moving through toddlerhood's incessant beckonings on to elementary's curiosity and adolescent arm-length askings, our children want our time and attention. And they need it because our time and attention affirm them. They

demand the setting aside of *us* for *them*. They insist on our undivided attention.

Dr. Ross Campbell defines "focused attention" as "giving a
child full, undivided attention in such a way that he feels without
doubt that he is completely loved. That he is valuable enough *in
his own right* to warrant parents' undistracted watchfulness, ap-
preciation, and uncompromising regard. In short, focused attention makes a child feel he
is the most important
person in the world in his
parents' eyes."[3]

*I notice that if my children don't get
enough attention, or are not told and
shown that they are loved and needed, they
tend to rebel or do something so they will
receive that attention. Also, my children
might act whiny or weepy over trivial
things if time passes without their getting
attention.*

— 🙚 —

Most moms recog-
nize the importance of
giving their child their
undivided attention. But
we struggle with finding
the time to do it. Many
of the moms surveyed for
this book responded that their children's greatest need was for
"my attention." Several described scenarios similar to this one.

"One day recently, three-year-old Jenny and I were eating
lunch together," wrote one mom. "She was chattering away
about the adventures of her morning at preschool. I was nod-
ding and saying, 'Uh huh,' but I was distracted by other
thoughts. Before I knew it, she got off her chair, came around
the table, climbed up on my lap, cupped my head in her hands,
and turned my face until we were exactly nose-to-nose.
'Mommy, I need your eyes,' she told me. I got her point."

It may seem obvious, but children need us to stop and
watch when they ask for our attention. They need our eyes and
our arms and our ears. During lap time and game time and talk
time and lunchtime. We know this, but we have a hard time car-

rying it out because of the price. "Paying" attention often means just that. It costs us our time.

The biggest obstacle to responding to our children's need for Crazy-About-Me Love is busyness. We face the tyranny of the urgent, those tasks that are not more important than our children, but that somehow grab our attention first. The dirty floor. The telephone calls. The regular television show. The committee report for next week's meeting.

Five years from now, what will you remember most? What will matter most? Sometimes we have to stop and ask ourselves these questions to gain perspective about our priorities. Perspective comes when we're able to see the bigger picture, or greater purpose, and fit the moment of today into that bigger picture of tomorrow, as Susan Lenzkes points out in this prayer called "Now."

> Lord,
> give me the sense to
> love,
> appreciate,
> and spend precious time
> with my children
> now
> so that someday
> I won't feel the need to
> smother my grandchildren
> with attention
> that belonged to
> their parents.[4]

That hits home, doesn't it? Our homes. It also hits our hearts. Our children's need for Crazy-About-Me Love is met with our time and attention, given carefully and consistently. Now, because today is when they need it.

Listening and Telling

In a survey of 250 children, ages 4 to 17, almost all said they wished their families had better communication.[5] Our children want and need communication with us, so how do we meet this need? Communication involves both listening and telling.

In his book *Seven Things Children Need,* John Drescher writes, "Listening carefully to the little hurts and complaints and joys of a child communicates real love."[6] So as moms, we need to resist the urge to edit, fill in the blanks, or interpret a child's words. We simply need to listen.

My four-year-old asked me to turn off the vacuum cleaner so I could hear him. He needed to know that I would play a game with him when I was done with my work.

— ❧ —

I am the queen of multi-tasking. I take great pride in being able to do more than one thing at a time, thus accomplishing twice as much. I struggle to lift my eyes from a good book to hear about the bus ride home. I'd rather peel the potatoes, baste the chicken, and listen to a report about a great test score than dry my hands and look at it page by page. It's difficult to tear away from the Figure Skating Championships on TV to show my daughter that I really do care if her two friends are still speaking to each other.

— ❧ —

After listening, we should use words as often as possible in praise. Praise is unique in its power to shape the personhood of a child. Goethe remarked, "In praising or loving a child, we love and praise not that which is, but that which we hope for." Similarly, August W. Hare commented, "The praises of others may be of use in teaching us not what we are, but what we ought to be." And Christian Bovec wrote, "Judicious praise is to children what the sun is to the flowers."

Praise has the power to shape our children! It works like a motivator, underlining what is already admirable in them and moving them to grow further in such qualities. One child development expert advised that children need ten "Attaboys" for every critical comment they are given. The power of positive words in our children's lives is a power we'd be wise to plug in to!

If you're interested in trying this game plan for affirming your little one, consider these suggestions:

1. Praise selectively. Indiscriminate praise doesn't motivate; it only confuses. When your child is disruptive or disrespectful, resist the myth that says they'll learn obedience by flattery. Praise only when behavior or character reflects your desires.

2. Praise immediately. Delayed praise has less meaning than immediate praise. When you praise a child hours after a good choice was made, he may not remember the action. Catch your little ones "in the act" of doing something praiseworthy, and then respond immediately.

3. Praise specifically. When you praise your child, assign your praise to noticeable acts or attitudes. "I like the way you shared your toy!" "What a good job you did on making your bed today!" "Look at you. You remembered to brush your teeth all by yourself!"

4. Praise intentionally. Look for ways to praise your child. When your daughter brings you a fingerpainting, look carefully for something you like in it (maybe the colors are mostly mud-like, but notice the smudge of bright yellow). Single out what you liked and then display the piece on the refrigerator or a bulletin board. When you're going about your daily chores and you notice

your toddler occupying himself with a puzzle, tell him how proud you are of his choice to play alone sometimes.

Communication involves both listening and telling. Make sure you open both your ears and your mouth to your child's need for affirmation.

Kindness and Tenderness

Several years ago a book entitled *Random Acts of Kindness* soared to the best-seller list. Its success underlined our need in society for the heart-offered effort of kindness in our daily routine. Families also thrive on this demonstration of love. And children learn they are loveable when a mother demonstrates love by expressing her love in tender action.

How could you act out your love for your child today? A box of animal crackers slipped into the grocery cart and pulled out on the way home might be a spontaneous way to say "I love you." What else?

My children often come and stand in front of me with their faces pressed to my stomach, and I know they need their hug cups filled. Or when they seem tired and cranky and out of control, we'll take a time-out for hugs to rejuvenate ourselves.

— ❧ —

For my youngest (who verbally demands her "private time" with Mama), we have R & R (Rock and Read), where we read from her choice of a book or mine.

— ❧ —

"I love you with all my heart and brain," my child tells me. I tell him the same.

— ❧ —

- Make a batch of favorite cookies this afternoon.
- Draw a picture and leave it on a pillow after bedtime for a wake-up surprise.
- Pick a flower and put it in a vase on a bedroom night table.

- Stick a note in a backpack or lunch box.
- Create a picnic with a blanket on the floor in the family room on a rainy day.
- Stir "red hot" candies into applesauce and cook it for a red-hot treat.
- Complete a child's chore and leave a note saying so with "I love you" attached.
- Surprise your little one by showing up at preschool and taking her out to lunch.

Do you sometimes wonder whether these random acts of kindness make any real difference in your child's life? MOPS International published a collection of drawings and one-line descriptions from preschool-aged children about what makes their moms special in a book entitled *Mommy, I Love You Just Because . . .* Their answers confirm that a mother's little acts of kindness zoom right to a child's heart and etch a forever-message of love. Here are samples of their comments:

My mom looks at me with love in her eyes.

My mom makes me the biggest, biggest dinner.

My mom looks at the clouds with me.

My mom and I run in the grass together.

My mom takes me to the zoo.

My mom gives me cozy hugs.

My mom took me on the Twister, and we went round and round together.

My mom helps me do things, like fold socks.

My mom plays checkers with me.

My mom helps me find things.[7]

As you act out your love for your child in kindnesses, also include the "tender treatment." How often we slip a tone of impatience, harsh criticism, or even degrading inferences into our interactions. Unwittingly, we sometimes make a joke to someone else at our child's expense.

"Your daughter is so adorable," a woman tells a mom as they wait in line at a fast food restaurant. The mother is holding her tired three-year-old in her arms.

"Cute?" the mother responds. "You should have seen her at 2 o'clock this morning. She wasn't a bit cute. I'd have given her to you in a gnat's breath!"

Everyone laughs . . . except the three-year-old girl, who has a wounded look on her face. She doesn't understand why her mother wanted to give her away in the middle of the night when she had a tummy ache.

Family expert Gary Smalley advises, "Children need to be treated tenderly. . . . Harshness and angry lecturing communicate to children that they are of little value and in some cases worthless. The phrase, 'If I meant anything to anyone, they wouldn't be so mean to me' is the frequent subconscious conclusion."[8]

When we lose our tempers, we need to apologize for our words. When we're impatient, we need to stop, take a deep breath, evaluate why, and remind ourselves of what really matters. If we make a mistake, we need to admit it. If we want cooperation, we need to win it through love. We need to lower our voices to a softer and gentler tone. When we do, it's amazing how quickly we are heard by our children.

Kind acts and tender treatment are simple but convincing ways to affirm the little ones we love so much. In her book *The New Boss Has*

My oldest son, with whom I tend to be very strict and sometimes harsh, said, "Mommy, I like your 'bedtime-story voice' because it's soft and sweet. How come you usually just use it when you read stories?"

— ❧ —

---

a Milk Mustache, Leola Floren processes her transition from the workforce to home and mothering. She describes the importance of these little acts of kindness and tenderness, which are sewn together like a quilt in a child's life. "Perhaps the most important lesson of a quilt," she writes, " is that no scrap, however small, is ever wasted or unimportant. That is the lesson of motherhood. Every hour spent reading fairy tales or Bible stories to a toddler is worthwhile and of lasting value. Every lunch of peanut butter on toast or peanut butter on celery or peanut butter on the kitchen floor is one more piece in the fabric that will eventually form the quilt of a person's childhood."[9]

My daughter had gotten into some trouble, and even though I was terribly disappointed in her, I told her how much I loved her. She told me later that my love was what turned her thinking around and made her decide to change.

— ❧ —

Advocacy

One other vital affirming tool is advocacy. An advocate is someone who pleads the case of another, one who stands in support. As mothers, we need to stand as advocates for our children by seeing the world through their eyes. In offering such "cheerleading" support, we convince them of their loveableness. One slight word of caution, however: Sometimes advocacy is appropriate; sometimes it is not.

After a particularly "challenging" morning, my then four-year-old and I were lying down before his nap. As we reviewed his less-than-ideal behavior, he looked at me and asked, "But you still love me, don't you, Mom?"

— ❧ —

When is advocacy appropriate?

- When your child is physically hurt by another.
- When a teacher misunderstands your child's needs.
- When your child is struggling to learn and needs to be tested or evaluated.
- When your child has physical or emotional symptoms of need.
- When your child confides a concern and needs help.
- When your child has been wrongly accused.
- When your child needs help expressing himself.
- When your child doesn't have the skills necessary to be an advocate for herself.

When is advocacy inappropriate? When it becomes the blind belief that your child can "do no wrong." Or when it is expressed as an irrational or obnoxious attitude that "my child would never hit another child" or "my child would never talk back to a teacher." Appropriate advocacy requires a truthful understanding of your child and an objective view of the current circumstances. Only then can you represent him and his best interests before others. When handled appropriately, moms who learn to be advocates for their children offer a kind of affirmation that helps convince those children that eventually they can become advocates for themselves.

GETTING TO THE HEART
OF CRAZY-ABOUT-ME LOVE

A child needs affirmation. He needs to know that he is loveable; she needs to know that you are crazy about her—no matter what. And children need to be reminded of this message again and again. When a mother mirrors this message consistently, with her time and attention, listening and telling, and kindness and tenderness, she imprints an eternal message on the heart of her child. This message will give that child the courage and confidence to face the world—and the children in the neighborhood who might hurt her feelings.

Love Handles

LOVE HANDLE #1:

More Spontaneous Acts of Affirmation
Words

- Nine Honest Ways to Say "Good for You":
  "That's quite an improvement."
  "Now you've got the hang of it."
  "I appreciate what you've done."
  "I can tell you really care."
  "I'm glad that you're my daughter/son."
  "What neat work!"
  "That's a good point."
  "You are so helpful."
  "Thanks for sharing."
- Use an affectionate nickname or pet name for your child. Make up new ones.
- Talk about when she was a tiny baby and how much you loved and wanted her.
- On Mother's Day, thank your child for giving you the opportunity to be a mother.
- Ask for your child's opinion more often.
- Let her hear you bragging about her.
- Thank him for little things.

Actions

- Play "I love you" games.
  Ask your child, "Guess how much I love you . . ."
  (Suggested answers, with hand motions: higher than
  the highest mountain, deeper than the deepest ocean,
  wider than the wide-blue-sky, taller than a tower made
  of all the Legos in the whole world.)

  Tell your child, "I wouldn't trade you for . . ." (Suggested answers: all the chocolate in all the candy stores
  in the world, all the stars in the sky, all the jelly beans in
  Wal-Mart, any other child in the whole wide world.)
- Show up at preschool with special snacks for everyone
  (check with the preschool teacher first).
- Take your child out of school or day care and out to
  lunch on his or her birthday.
- Put smiley face stickers in random places, as a reminder
  message that "you put a smile in my heart."
- Read books aloud; take the child to the library and let
  him choose which books to check out.
- Out of the clear blue, have an "I love_____" dinner,
  with a centerpiece that specially honors your child,
  and spend the mealtime talking about the reasons you
  love her.
- Take one child at a time on an errand. After doing the
  errand, end up at an ice cream store for sundaes and a
  special time together.
- On a Saturday morning, ask your child, "What would
  you like to do today?" Then do it.
- Plan a weekend trip. Describe all the possibilities, then
  let your child choose the destination.
- Fly kites together.
- Build lots of blanket forts.

- Walk barefoot through a mud puddle together if she suggests it.
- Put his art creation on the refrigerator door.
- Plant a kiss in the palm of her hand so she can carry it around all day.

LOVE HANDLE #2:

Ten Ways You Can Shape a Child's Life

- Notice him. Mention something about him that you see, or acknowledge his presence in some way.
- Encourage him. Help him develop a natural ability. "I knew you could do that."
- Listen to him. Give him your undivided attention.
- Inquire about his plans for the future. Such questions cause the child to feel that there is someone who is really interested in him and may start a flow of thought toward the future.
- Let him ask you questions. Most people who ask a question are not so much seeking an answer as a chance to talk about the subject. Lead the child to talk further rather than giving a pat answer.
- Lift up ideals before him. Children are natural hero worshipers. It's never too early to bolster their admiration for people who have done noble things in their lifetime.
- Compliment him. This will assure him of your love and concern.
- Share from your own life experience. "Let me tell you what happened to me once" helps more than a lecture.
- Tell him about God. The greatest influence we can have on a child is for eternity. We can give him hope.[10]

LOVE HANDLE #3:

Diagnosing "Busy Mom" Disease

Here's a "busyness" test to give you a lighter look at the distractions you face.

__ Not Busy: Your toddler is fully dressed in clothes that match.

__ Busy: Your toddler is wearing a diaper and shirt.

__ Too Busy: Your toddler is wearing a diaper—and it probably needs changing.

__ Not busy: Your laundry is washed, dried, folded, and put away.

__ Busy: Your laundry is clean, but it's still in laundry baskets.

__ Too busy: Your family's dirty clothes never made it to the laundry room.

__ Not busy: Your children's toys are neatly stashed away and the carpet is vacuumed.

__ Busy: Toys are scattered in the vicinity of the toy box.

__ Too busy: You're so exhausted that you let building blocks, tanks, and cowboys lie wherever they fell.[11]

LOVE HANDLE #4:

A Mother's Timesaving Tips

A mother often asks herself, "Where did this day go? I need more extra minutes to spend time with my children!" Here are some simple timesaving tips to help you find more minutes in your day:

- Turn off the television. Pick one program a day to watch; otherwise, turn off the television. When it's on, we often get hooked into a program that eats up another hour of the day.

- Systematize any regular jobs, like: (1) Laundry—use plastic baskets to sort by color or use one basket for each child; (2) Dishes—everyone helps to clear the table, scrapes and washes their own dishes, and puts them in the dishwasher, not in the sink; (3) Mail—read and sort next to the wastebasket. Handle each piece only once. Dispose of junk mail immediately. Have a "home" for catalogs you will use, such as a wicker basket.
- Find a "place for everything." Invest in some plastic containers and file cabinets and get organized by designating regular homes for things like coupons, recipes, shopping lists, car keys, checkbooks, photographs, and important papers such as car titles, birth certificates, and health records. When you have a place for things, cleanup is faster, and you spend less time looking for things.
- Combine errands. Think ahead and combine your errands on certain days to prevent running all over town.
- Eliminate unnecessary work. Find one task in your routine that you can give up because it doesn't matter so much! If one doesn't come to mind, talk with another mother and together come up with one for each of you. Then hold each other accountable to stopping. It may be vacuuming the living room every day (because you like the look of the "vacuum lines" on the carpet). Or ironing the sheets. Or traveling to four different grocery stores to find bargains, when one stop might save more in time and gasoline. Intentionally work at eliminating unrealistic expectations of yourself or compulsive habits.
- Do it right the first time. Take the extra minutes to sew a button on tightly, so it will last. Stock up on frequently used items on sale to save running back to the store. Make doubles of casseroles or cookies and freeze some.

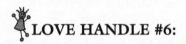

LOVE HANDLE #5:

When to Say Yes Instead of No

Here are some ways to keep you from overcommitment and freer to meet your child's needs:

Say yes when:

- You've taken time to think about it. Your first response might not be the best response. Consider the cost to you personally. What will you give up to take on this responsibility? Sleep? Another commitment? The ability to respond to your family's needs?
- Your family's needs have been considered and you have their support. Certain seasons or stages demand more of you than other seasons and stages.
- The task uses your skills and gives you a sense of joy in serving.
- The task teaches you a new skill or stretches you in a direction you want to grow.
- You're not doing it out of a sense of guilt or because you fear disappointing someone else.

LOVE HANDLE #6:

Redefining "Quality Time" with Children

Too often, we hear the term "quantity vs. quality," which is supposed to help us evaluate the time we spend with our children. The idea is that it isn't how *much* time is spent with a child, but the *kind* of time that matters. Author Valerie Bell tackles this subject in her book *Getting Out of Your Kids' Faces and into Their Hearts.* "If you want to spend quality time with your child," she writes, " you need to be available *when they need you.*" Quality time is not a weekend here, a vacation there. "Quality time is the consistent daily sharing of life with your children. Quality time is the time spent in meeting your child's needs."

Here are some of the examples of quality time Bell gives:

- Quality time is volunteering to be the room mother or a chaperone for a field trip.
- Quality time is when your child can't sleep at night, and you're available to comfort and soothe his anxieties.
- Quality time is when your kid has friends over, and you're around to enjoy them.
- Quality time is laughing at each other's jokes.
- Quality time is getting to know your child so well that you can anticipate and meet his or her needs.[12]

MOM READING:

The Blessing, John Trent
Getting Out of Your Kids' Faces and Into Their Hearts, Valerie Bell
How to Really Love Your Child, Ross Campbell, M.D.
The Key to Your Child's Heart, Gary Smalley
Little House on the Freeway, Tim Kimmel
Mommy, I Love You Just Because . . . , MOPS International
Perfect Every Time: When Doing It all Leaves You with Nothing, Paula
   Rinehart
The Power of a Parent's Words, H. Norm Wright

LAP READING:

Corduroy, Don Freeman
Guess How Much I Love You? Sam McBratney
I'd Choose You! John Trent
I Love You As Much . . . , Laura Krauss Melmed
The Kissing Hand, Audrey Penn
Mama, Do You Love Me? Barbara M. Joosse

Three

Belonging:
Fit-Me-Into-the-Family Love

Kate pulled the thread tightly into a knot, lifted it to her teeth, and bit it off. Holding her work out at an arms-length, she examined the stitches on the fancy Christmas stocking. They spelled out the first two letters of the name "Hannah." Only a week left, and she had to have it finished.

Baby Hannah had surprised them all, hatching into the family six weeks early. Kate had planned her arrival to be *post-*Christmas! And now she had so much to do, in addition to meeting the needs of her tiny, premature baby. Her parents had planned to come for the holidays anyway, so they came out a bit early. They'd been lifesavers, especially with five-year-old Brendon, who loved Grandma and Grandpa.

But ever since she'd come home from the hospital with Hannah, Brendon seemed starved for her undivided attention. Earlier, he had begged her to sit by him while he watched television. Since the baby and Grandma and Grandpa were all napping, she got out the sewing basket and stocking project and sat beside him on the couch. He now snuggled close beside her, watching cartoons and her progress on the stocking.

"Why do you have to make a stocking for Hannah, Mommy? She can't open any presents. She won't even know she has a stocking. She's too little. So what's the big deal anyway?"

"Hannah's part of the family now, just like you are, Brendon," Kate answered, putting her arm around him. "And you know that everyone in our family has a Christmas stocking, even Grandma and Grandpa. Even if Hannah isn't big enough to know she has a stocking this Christmas, when she gets older she'll see this stocking in the pictures we take on Christmas morning and she'll know we were so glad to have her in our family. You know how you love all those pictures of your first Christmas when you were a new baby."

Brendon didn't seem impressed. "Well, I think this family is getting too big," he said with a glum sigh as he returned his attention to the cartoons.

Just then Kate heard Hannah whimpering. Because she was small, she needed more time and attention than an average newborn. And her needs required the whole family to take special precautions. Washing hands. More rocking. Most difficult was staying indoors, away from people and the exciting holiday happenings at the malls and church. Kate's own energy level was waning from complications at Hannah's birth and the many nights of lost sleep. She still had shopping to do for Brendon ... and wrapping ... and baking ... and, and, and! The list was endless.

"Mommy, where are you going?" came Brendon's insistent question as she got up to feed Hannah. Kate sighed, but then heard the sounds of Grandma rattling some pots and pans in the kitchen. "Brendon, my boy," Grandma called out. "Can you come here and help me get these cookies going! I can't manage this recipe without my big helper!"

"Ah, Hannah, dear," Kate cooed to her tiny baby as she scooped her up out of the bassinet. "We'll handle all this. There will be enough of me and Dad and Grandma and Grandpa and even enough of Brendon for you, precious child. We can all fit into this family."

A PLACE CALLED "BELONG"

Children need a sense of belonging. They need a place and a space to call their own. They need to know they fit into a family that surrounds them with a love that moves over and makes room for them. We hear this yearning expressed best by orphaned or abandoned children. "I want to be in a family where I can stay and belong," a six-year-old recently said on a television program that focused on children waiting for adoption.

As moms, we have the most natural opportunity to meet our children's need for belonging. As Drs. Henry Cloud and John Townsend express in their book *The Mom Factor*, "We all

Busyness is a problem. As a mom, I shuffle myself and my children from work to meetings to classes. We all live in the same house, but we don't always live as a family.

— ❧ —

have a need to belong to someone and to something bigger than ourselves. Belonging and love are at the root of our humanness. ... And it is our mother's responsibility to rescue us from alienation and isolation and to usher us into the world of relationship."[1]

Family Stretch Marks

Making room for a new child in the family is a challenge that requires all family members to adjust. Just like a mother's body expands and rearranges itself to accommodate the needs of a baby growing within, so when the baby is born and comes home to live, the family must make room to accommodate the new addition. In the beginning, the transition makes special demands on family members, which require some sacrifices, but an infant picks up on the "family vibes" and needs to feel welcomed rather than rejected or resented. The way she is held and nurtured communicates the message of belonging.

Mom's Stretch Marks

A family has to adjust, and so does Mom. But while pregnancy had its own demands, the transition to home life can be even harder. Sometimes we wonder if we can really meet our child's need for Fit-Me-Into-the-Family Love.

"I need some space for me!"

Babies, toddlers, and children take up so much *room!* Their stuff is everywhere. Before they were around, we could keep things straight. But now, well, there's always such a mess! We used to know that our purse would be on the kitchen counter, our brush in the bathroom, our scissors in the kitchen drawer. Now the search for each item becomes a treasure hunt, eating up valuable time and energy. Make room in the family? We want to, but it seems that when we make room for our child, we're shoved into the corners both physically and emotionally.

Space for you may be rare, but it can be found when you look for it. Teach your older preschoolers to have a "quiet time" each day where each of you can spend time alone. Ask your husband for an evening each week—for you alone. Trade babysitting with a friend and spend time alone in *your* house. It's okay for us to need and take space for ourselves. This can actually make us better moms!

"I have more than one child. How do I love them equally?"

I was so busy doing other activities like housework and caring for my two-year-old that the only time I had given my older daughter was when she was home sick and no other children were there.

— ❧ —

Somehow, amazingly, love grows alongside a baby within our wombs. And equally as awesomely, that love is born in our hearts when they are born. The plain fact is that we *can* love more than one child—a lot. Some mothers understand this concept by using the analogy of a candle. The mother's love is like the flame of a candle. As each child is born, she gives them her love by lighting each of their candles. But giving away her love never diminishes her flame. She always has enough to share.

But meeting each child's needs in the same manner may be more difficult. As moms, we need to let go of the self-imposed pressure to do for one what we did for another. Such guilt usually holds us back from offering the love we can give. Instead of fretting over not doing

After having three boys, we had a girl. Our second boy, Eric, said to me, "Mommy, why do you love Nikki more than you love us?" I immediately assured him that I loved him just as much as I did Nikki. I told him that it only seemed like I loved her more because she was a baby and had more needs than he did at that time. Then I assured him that this was the case with a big hug and kiss.

— ❧ —

it "the way you did it before," invest your attention in asking, "What does this child need from me now?" and then give it.

"How do I fit an adopted child into the family?"

Whether adopted at infancy or later in life, adopted children need special measures to fit them into the family. Moms can feel especially insecure about their preparedness and adequacy and may need extra encouragement both from husbands and friends. Here are some suggestions for fitting your adopted child into your family:

- Touch your baby through holding him, wearing him in a sling or front pack, and through infant massage. Touch is key in bonding, and both you and your baby need extra amounts of touch as you bond.
- Honor your child's birth parentage. Perhaps you have an open adoption where you are in communication

with your child's birth parents. Maybe it was closed, and you know very little. Design for your child an "adoptive baby book" that holds her birth history and other information. When she has questions, read through this book together.

- Pay close attention to your feelings as an adoptive mother. Fears of abandonment and rejection are common for many adoptive moms as they picture their children processing their relationship with their birth parents. Be honest with yourself about your feelings and seek help processing them if needed.

- Get to know your child. Find out all you can about your child's biological history. Did his parents graduate from high school? Are there health concerns you should know? Approach your child with the attitude that he is a present you get to help unwrap. While all children are discoveries to their parents, adopted children benefit from this mind-set.

The Benefits of Family Room

Making room for a new family member results in many benefits to the child. First, the sense of belonging brings to a child a stability that grows with her through all the ages and stages of life. When children feel like they fit within a family, their value and worth are validated, and they are able to offer that same sense of stability to other relationships in the larger world in which they live. As John Drescher writes in his reflective book *If I Were Starting My Family Again*, "When children feel they belong in the family and are of real worth there, they enter the world strong, feeling loved and accepted, and with the ability to love and accept others."[2]

They also begin to build a reservoir of strength upon which they can draw in difficult times. A group of children who had lost both parents in World War II were studied to determine their ability to go on after the war. Those

> *I look for opportunities to allow my children to make contributions. This past week I let my boys help me with a mailing I was doing at work. They needed to sort, fold, put labels on envelopes, stamp them, and sort them for in and out of town. It was a great help to me and they felt very important.*
>
> — ❧ —

who remembered doing many things together as a family were best able to pick up and begin again.[3]

Second, the feeling of belonging contributes to a child's physical health and sense of well-being. Studies increasingly show the feelings that come from loving or being loved are linked with higher levels of antibodies or cells that fight infection in the body. Further, the feeling of belonging also seems to reduce stress chemicals in the body.[4] In other words, fitting family members into the family makes everybody healthier.

FAMILY LIFE

A child's need for belonging is met in the family structure. To build a family with room for all, consider certain blueprints in the construction.

Home as a Haven

"There's no place like home!" Dorothy whispered as she journeyed back from Oz to her home in Kansas. Ahhh. We all know the truth and comfort of that statement. It means walking in the front door and smelling a savory soup that's been simmering on the stove, or the scent of freshly baked cookies that tells us someone has prepared for our arrival! It means sitting in a circle on the floor in front of the fireplace, playing games and laughing together. It means Saturday morning snuggles in bed or celebrating family birthdays with balloons at breakfast.

A good home underlines and emphasizes the belonging of all who enter. Like a welcome mat that pronounces a greeting, this home ushers all members safely inside where they can be re-fueled and refreshed for living in the everyday world. Children cling to the idea of home as a haven and place of nurture, and they delight in explaining what "home" means to them.

"Home is the place you go when it gets dark," one child explained.

"Home is the place where people love you no matter what happens," according to another. "Home is the place you can scratch . . . no matter where it itches."

Maintaining the physical place called home is a challenge these days. Jobs, sports, even hobbies often take a higher prior-ity in some families. Child advocate Marian Wright Edelman emphasizes the importance of a home. "Parents for today's chil-dren must at all cost maintain a home, a center of love for their nurture and security. The pressure of our high-powered civi-lization is too much for a homeless and loveless child. . . . *Noth-ing* must separate parents from their duty to their children."[5]

The perception of home as a haven is greatly affected by the quality of the relationships in the home, especially the rela-tionship between the mother and father. Child and family ex-pert John Drescher observes, "Knowing parents love each other provides children with a security, stability, and sacredness about life that they can gain in no other way. . . . If true love is not demonstrated at home, they pick up false ideas about love from movies, novels, and magazines. . . . Children need to see gen-uine love modeled by their parents."[6]

When children are deprived of this relational modeling that makes home a haven, they try to fill their need by finding that security else-

Our children need to know that their daddy and I love each other and that we will always be there for them.

— ♠ —

where. Sometimes siblings attempt to meet this need for each other. A small article in a local newspaper described such a situation recently. It seems that a six-year-old boy brought his five-year-old sister to school, even though the little girl did not attend that school. When the teacher investigated, she discovered that the mother was an alcoholic who had passed out on the couch, and the little boy did not want to leave his young sister alone. Older children often seek a sense of haven with friends when they do not find it in their own homes.

Families of All Designs

Not all families look alike. Some include married parents, and others single parents. Some boast an only child while others have multiple siblings. Some are built by blood, and others through adoption. Still others extend their boundaries to include several generations, bringing in Grandma and Grandpa or Aunt Sally. Whatever the makeup of your family, recognize it for what it is: a family! Built of varying backgrounds and ancestry, and uniquely woven together with layers of love, families are a God-designed structure, intended to be a haven and meet the need for Fit-Me-Into-the-Family Love.

In her book *What Good Parents Have in Common*, Janis Long Harris writes that "the kind of family children need in order to grow up healthy is more than the nuclear family. . . . Children benefit tremendously from immersion in extended family life. Close relationships with grandparents . . . neighbors, and even business colleagues. Strong friendships. Hospitality. Affiliation with institutions made up of people who share your strongly held convictions."[7]

BUILDING IN BELONGING

Most often, moms take charge of designing, building, and strengthening this sense of belonging in children. We are the "construction site managers" on the homefront. But we also have lots of tools at our disposal. Through the remainder of this chapter, you'll find many ideas that will help you in constructing a family that communicates a sense of belonging to the children who are growing up in it!

Parental Legacies

You have a personal history to offer your child; including him in yours will help him build his own. Pull your little ones up on your lap and open up the storybook of your own life. Share with them how you grew up: what kind of house you lived in, your customs, your struggles, your most embarrassing moments, your dreams of what you thought you'd be. Remember that a single telling is seldom enough. Children learn best through repetition, when the same lessons are applied again and again in different corners of their lives.

Other ideas for sharing your own legacy include taking your children to visit the town where you grew up. Walk together down the street where you lived. Take them to your first school, past the grocery store or church, and to your favorite park. Share your memories from each spot. Teach them your favorite childhood game. Show them pictures. If appropriate, tell them when and how you met their daddy. Tell them your love story. Describe your wedding to them.

Some families have visual aids that identify the history, character, and unity of the family, like a name for their homestead or a family "coat of arms." In times past, a family coat of arms used symbols to depict the qualities of a particular family, such as flowers to symbolize virtues or animals to symbolize strength. You could make up your own family's coat of arms to symbolize the character of your family.

The Gifts of Grandparents

Grandparents offer many gifts to a family. If your children's grandparents live far away, consider "adopting" grandparents in your neighborhood. Their influence is important, so receive them eagerly and with joy!

- Grandparents provide family culture. The family's history is deepened and lengthened with the inclusion of a grandparent's legacy. They reinforce family traditions and make them more fun.
- Grandparents offer perspective. Because they've "been there and done that," grandparents take life less seriously and have a better perspective about what really matters in the bigger picture of life.
- Grandparents give us a break. They often offer a helping hand, which gives us an opportunity to relax and stop sweating the small stuff.
- Grandparents build bridges. They help two very different generations come together on common ground. Because they don't have a "stake" in winning many of the power games of parenting, they can offer insight and a path to peace.
- Grandparents open us to compassion. Watching those we love grow old changes us and provides us with opportunities to understand aging and need in the grand

scope of human life. Exposing children to the needs of their grandparents gives them the chance to reach outside of themselves to love.

Once our son told us he wanted to go live with his retired grandparents, who give him lots of undivided attention.

— ✿ —

If we accept the idea that kids can never receive too much Fit-Me-Into-the-Family Love, then including grandparents in our extended family multiplies a child's opportunities to experience love and acceptance.

Chore-Sharing

While it may not be the most popular, one of the most effective tools for creating a sense of belonging in a child is the opportunity to pitch in and contribute to the family by doing chores. Work is family stuff. When you assign responsibilities, even to small children, you communicate that they are valued and needed in order for the family to continue on. As much as kids seem to resist responsibilities, deep down they need to know they are counted on. Yet they often need help in learning how to tackle their chores, and those chores need to be age-appropriate.

Robert Barnes, in *Raising Confident Kids*, suggests four steps in helping children with chores: example, exposure, experience, and encouragement. Examples of appropriate chores for young children include making their beds, unloading the plastic containers from the dishwasher, putting away their clothes, setting the table, and caring for a pet. All these daily activities provide proof that they fit into the family and that the family depends upon them and needs their help.

Sibling Loyalties and Sacrifices

A sense of belonging also grows out of the development of sibling loyalties and the understanding that not all siblings are treated equally all the time. When a new baby enters the family, for instance, a three-year-old sibling learns that new babies need lots of immediate attention. That's how it was when he entered the family three years earlier, and that's how it is now for his new little sister. In this transition, he will learn that his mother's love for him has not changed; that's simply the way life is in a family.

I try to offer my older child an alternative time if I'm busy and she wants me for something. I may say, "Let Mom finish bathing the baby and then you and I will read together."

— ❧ —

Several months before the birth of my son, my five-year-old daughter and I were clothes shopping for him. She kept choosing outfits and asking me if I liked them. We made some choices and purchased them. One outfit that she picked out I almost did not buy. Later she asked me if she had picked good colors. I didn't understand what she was talking about until she said, "Mommy, you weren't going to buy the clothes I picked out." I had to secretly ask my husband to ooh and aah over the outfit she picked to build her back up. And when the baby was born, I made a big deal out of it every time he wore her outfit.

— ❧ —

Siblings and parents make sacrifices for each other. A mother bringing a new baby home helps a toddler make this adjustment by spending extra special time with the older child to meet his needs. The toddler begins to understand that his mother needs to meet different children's needs at different times, which means not every child is treated equally all the time. It's part of the reality of belonging in a family where everyone learns to sacrifice for each other. Helping a child learn this lesson prepares the child for life out in the world where treatment is not always "fair" or "equal."

Traditions!

Traditions can form the framework (and often the fun!) of the family. Just as framing uniquely shapes a house in the building process, traditions also uniquely shape and support the identity for a family. Historically, traditions have preserved families through tumultuous times. Immigrants to America brought customs, rituals, and traditions to mark important events in family life. Without material wealth, culture decorated their homes. Special family recipes held them together around tables. Following World War II, as mobility and divorce fragmented families, many of these longstanding traditions began to lose their importance.

Today it is vital that families use the tool of tradition to build a sense of belonging. Dr. James Dobson comments, "The great value of traditions is that they give a family a sense of identity, of belonging ... that we're not just a cluster of people living together in a house, but we're a family that's conscious of its uniqueness, of its personality, of its character, and its heritage."[8]

But how? How do we build traditions into our newly formed families? Follow this guideline: Choose traditions from your past that have had special meaning for you, establish new ones for your own family today, and let go of traditions that have lost their meaning. Come together as a family to talk through which rituals have meaning and which do not. Blend practices from both sides of the family. Encourage your children to say what they like and don't like and then take their opinions to heart. When we learn to hold traditions loosely, they can shape our family rather than control it.

Family traditions can be built upon everyday events. Some families have a tradition of making a new message for their answering machine every season. Each member takes turns shaping or speaking the message. A simple but creative phone message also gives a message about a family and the importance of every family member.

Many family traditions are built around special holidays and celebrations. Some families spontaneously celebrate the first snow of the season with a special dinner. Just as anniversaries, Flag Day, and the Fourth of July have their own annual rituals, family traditions shape a family and build a sense of belonging.

Birthdays

A child thrives on the realization that one day out of the year is totally his. His birthday is the day he gets to call the shots, request the dinner menu, and feel just plain special all day long. The day might start by waking the birthday boy or girl (or mom or dad!) with a birthday crown, a candle bedecked cake, and a serenade. Pull out the baby book and retell the birthday child's story—what time he was born or when he was brought home in adoption, his first words, smiles, or other memories of when he was little. Encourage each family member to share a quality they particularly appreciate about the birthday person. Serve a favorite meal. Make cupcakes together. Hide the presents and send the birthday person on a treasure hunt to find them.

Thanksgiving

Have each family member or guest around the table share something for which he is thankful. Tell favorite jokes and prod one another to laugh. Enlist the help of each child in the preparation of one dish. This can become a yearly ritual. (Benjamin's mashed potatoes, Meagan's jello salad, etc.) Make a Thanksgiving tree for the birds with birdseed ornaments. Have a pie-eating contest. Help serve meals at a soup kitchen.

Christmas

For most families, Christmas is the holiday with traditions that stretch out over the longest period of time. Some start the day after Thanksgiving with shopping. Next it's posing for the family Christmas card picture. Then there's the tree selection and decorating. In a month-long period of celebration, find the balance in selecting traditions that work for your family. Blend customs from both Mom's and Dad's sides of the family. Celebrate the twelve days of Christmas with a tiny trinket each day. Give each child a tree ornament each year. (Later these can be taken to their own adult homes.) Include the history of St. Nicholas along with the traditional meaning of Christmas. Practice Advent the four weeks prior to Christmas, and trace the developments surrounding the birth of Jesus. Hold a "It's Jesus' birthday" party for neighbors and share with them the meaning of Christmas. Select favorite foods and make them year after year.

Reunions

Reunions give children a great sense of the history and the knowledge of their extended family. Plan well in advance. Purchase inexpensive T-shirts for all family members to wear with a catchy family-themed slogan. Rent a church camp or other campground and cook, sleep, and play together. Create a photo memory book or a videotape from the days together for each family to take home. Honor the eldest and youngest members of the family with a poem, a small gift, or a story. Audio tape the histories of the older members to pass down to those yet to come.

Mealtime

One of the simplest ways to maintain a sense of family unity and belonging is to sit around a table together for a meal. Since plenty of distractions eat away at this family tradition, you need to be intentional—and often sacrifice other things—to make it work. So turn off the TV. Set the table with candles. Make conversation the focus of the meal. Keep the comments positive. Involve each family member. Take turns cooking. Hold hands and say grace together, alternating who prays each time. Enlist children in preparation and cleanup.

Bedtime

Children love bedtime routines. Getting tucked into bed makes a child feel loved and nurtured. No wonder children ritualize and stretch out those routines with their requests to follow the same pattern each night. Taking a warm bath. Brushing their teeth. Reading a bedtime story. Saying their prayers. Having a drink of water. Listening to a lullaby. Getting hugs and smooches. Having another drink of water. Getting tucked in. Turning the night-light on. Having just one more drink of water. Calling "night-night" down the hall. (Beware of all that water! Too many drinks will get you out of bed later with another request in the middle of the night. Besides, that repeated request is often just a stall technique, aimed at stretching out the bedtime ritual because it is so much fun!) Enlist Dad and let him offer his own ingredients to the routine. Teach babysitters to follow the same sequence.

We tell our baby-sitter, "First the kids brush their teeth, then we read them a story, then we have them say their prayers." This emphasizes how our family does things.

— ✿ —

Everyday practices

Develop some "the way we do it" routines. Good-morning kisses. Breakfast Bible readings. Saturday morning chores. Friday night family nights. First day of school pancakes. Last day of school picnic. Fall leaf rake. Labor Day family work day. Summer raspberry pick. April Fool's Day jokes. Car-trip games. Tooth Fairy notes and surprises.

Family keepsakes

The family archives or treasures help children feel a part of the family. Have an area where photo albums are stored and where they are easily accessible to kids. Buy sturdy albums so that the children can pull them out often and laugh at what they looked like as newborn babies. Have a collection of Christmas photo albums that you put out on the coffee table only in December. Keep family Christmas cards together in an album also. Keep a "treasure box" for each child, filled with personal keepsakes. Host a family video night several times a year and show the favorite family videos of last year's summer vacation or cousin John's graduation from high school. Kids get a sense of continuity in the family as they see themselves in these pictures and videos.

Religious rituals

In her book *Traits of a Healthy Family*, author Delores Curran says that a healthy family has a shared religious core, and religion strengthens family relationships.[9] Important milestones in a child's life are often built around the sharing of religious rituals. Holding hands and saying grace before meals. Going to church and Sunday school together and out to lunch afterward. Memorizing Sunday school Scriptures. Having a Tuesday night family worship. Finding Scripture notes on pillows. Saying nighttime prayers. Singing songs and hymns and going to choir practice. Giving gifts at Christmas to the less fortunate. Baking an Easter brunch for the neighborhood. Tracking family prayer requests in a journal. They all weave together to form part of this important framework.

GETTING TO THE HEART
OF FIT-ME-INTO-THE-FAMILY LOVE

Children hunger for a sense of belonging. They display it as soon as they impact the family with their arrival, their newborn needs demanding that family members make some adjustments and make room for them. As mothers, we often feel like construction site managers, in charge of this responsibility of making sure the baby feels welcomed into the family structure. We juggle responsibilities, family schedules, and baby feedings, so that the home will be a haven for all. As children grow up, we use the tools of family traditions and celebrations, reunions and special meals, chore charts and photograph albums. We build this sense of belonging in order to meet their need for Fit-Me-Into-the-Family Love.

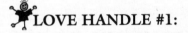

Love Handles

LOVE HANDLE #1:

Five Ways to Help Mom Overcome Her Own Childhood Issues

Don't let your own issues about belonging in a family interfere with your relationships with your children. If you need help:

1. Ask others for feedback.
2. Attend parenting classes.
3. Concentrate on your strengths in thoughtful prayer and meditation.
4. Ask for help from a friend or counselor.
5. If a problem continues for six months or more, seek professional help.[10]

LOVE HANDLE #2:

Family Photo Albums and Scrapbooks

One of the best ways to build a sense of family unity and belonging is to take lots of pictures and then keep a special album for your child. Save those treasures in a scrapbook that enables the child to enjoy those memories over and over again. Here are some suggestions about what to save and how to make scrapbooks or photograph albums that will last long enough to pass down to the next generation.

What to save:

Photographs. Get a camera that's simple to use, and then keep it loaded with film and in a convenient place. Try to capture candid moments. Get down on the floor and take pictures from a child's perspective. Sort through your pictures and identify them while the memories and dates are fresh in your mind. Use a rubber date stamp to date the back of the pictures as soon as you bring them home.

Letters. As a mom, get in the habit of writing letters to your child. Some moms start with personal letters, even before the child is born. Write a description of your child's birth and the first day of her life. (Believe it or not, you forget some of those vivid details!) You can also collect letters from grandparents, godparents, special friends, or preschool teachers.

Journal entries. Less formal than letters, journals can include those little reflections about your child, his humorous antics, responses from other people about him. Save other mementos such as artwork, notes, preschool reports, doctor's notes.

How to save the stuff:

- Save your child's treasures in a special box or file drawer until you can make a scrapbook. Even the box or file should be accessible to your child, so she can enjoy looking at "her" stuff.
- Use quality materials. Use pages that are acid-free and ones that lie flat while you are working on them.
- Use photo-safe adhesives to mount pictures and mementos such as ribbons, awards, and invitations. Avoid rubber cement, scotch tape, or staples as they will get discolored and eat through the treasured items.

- Crop pictures for creative use, but also to edit out whatever distracts from the main subject.
- Mat pictures by using acid-free paper. Regular construction paper is acidic and fades.
- Use an acid-free pen for identifying pictures and adding comments. The ink in regular ball-point pens or felt-tip pens will seep through the surface of the pictures.

LOVE HANDLE #3:

Good Times with Grandparents

Whether your children see their grandparents every week or once a year, family dynamics often create tension and stress when everyone is together. Here are some ways to diffuse possible conflicts before they arise:

- Allow your child to spend time alone with the grandparents. A connection between them is best forged on a one-to-one basis.
- Don't expect your parents always to agree with the way you are raising your children.
- When your parents give advice, attempt to listen graciously, even if you decide not to heed it.
- Keep your children on the sidelines of any conflict. Don't let them feel they are driving a wedge between their parents and grandparents.
- Let everyone take an occasional break. A trip to the grocery store or a walk with the kids might be the thing everyone needs when tension starts to mount.
- Keep communication open. Allow room for discussion on parenting styles and the role grandparents play in the lives of their grandchildren.[11]

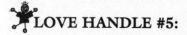

LOVE HANDLE #4:

Toys at Grandma's House

Grandparents often feel uncertain about what toys to provide for preschoolers these days. Here are some inexpensive suggestions (or ones you can bring along to get the visit started):

- Buckets of Duplo blocks with animals (Age 1 and up)
- Age-appropriate crayons and blank paper (Age 2 and up)
- Wooden train and track set (Ages 3–6)
- Dress-up box with old clothes and accessories (Ages 3–7)
- A cast of hand puppets (Age 4 and up)[12]

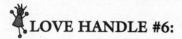

LOVE HANDLE #5:

Family Mealtime Fun with Kids

Have everybody bring something to the table for show and tell.

Have a "good news report" on something good you noticed about each child that day.

Let each child name one friend they'd like to invite over in the next couple of weeks.

Use candles and paper plates.

Listen to your kids talk.

Eat in the dining room.

LOVE HANDLE #6:

Everyday Celebrations

Look for some more ways to turn ordinary days into family celebrations. Here are some suggestions:

- First day of spring
- A good soccer game
- A pet's birthday
- Daylight savings ending
- Cinco de Mayo
- A made-up birthday, like Mickey Mouse's
- Get one of those calendars with all sorts of different celebrations noted

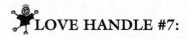

LOVE HANDLE #7:

Birthday Party Themes

Birthday parties are more fun—and actually easier for Mom, the hostess—when there's a theme to tie in decorations and games. Here are some suggestions:

My Hero

My Favorite Pet

My Favorite Insect

The Great Treasure Hunt

Clowning Around

LOVE HANDLE #8:

Memory Makers

Always be prepared to turn a regular day into a F.A.M.I.L.Y. celebration and time to make some memories:

F ilm and camera. Pictures make great memories. Take photos of new haircuts, special outfits, gingerbread houses about to be eaten, school projects, giveaway gifts you wish you could keep, Christmas festivities, and birthday events. Keep at least a couple of rolls of film on hand all the time, with extra camera batteries as well.

A ttitude of sensitivity. Know when to take pictures and when to just enjoy the moment. Pajama pictures don't go over well with self-conscious preteens. But those same preteens might feel devastated if you forget to take the annual sitting-in-the-wrapping-paper picture.

M anipulatives. These items help families be together without the pressure of entertaining each other. We work a new puzzle every Christmas season, a diversion that became a "we always do that" tradition when we did a puzzle two years in a row. Board games, plastic models, piano music, or brainteasers work for other families. Also try stitching quilts, painting T-shirts, or whittling wood. Keep on hand whatever your family members enjoy.

"I likes." Keep in mind the preferences of your family members as you do your routine errands. You might see everything you need for your father-in-law's favorite lasagna on sale six months before his birthday. Make him one and pop it in your freezer. When you come across a uniquely textured yarn, tuck it away for your daughter who weaves. All-year shopping spreads out the expense, makes it more likely that you'll find gifts that fit your family's personality, and heads off some of the rushed feelings of the holidays.

L ittle gifts. Keep on hand small stocking-stuffer type gifts that make a day special. My preschool-aged daughter once invented "Val-an-mas Day," a unique celebration that occurred during that long no-holiday stretch between Valentine's Day and Easter. Having inside information, she assured us that presents were a crucial part of the holiday. On-hand gifts equip you to celebrate Val-an-mas Days, good report cards, cooperative behavior during everybody-has-the-flu week, and much more. The few days following holidays are good times to find these gifts at half price or less.

Yummy dessert: Even if your freezer space is limited to the top part of your refrigerator, you can stash away a pan of frosted brownies or an ice cream pie. When a special day comes, you already have a cake to celebrate with. Once you eat it, replace it within a week.[13]

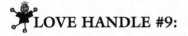**LOVE HANDLE #9:**

Make Your Own Family Coat of Arms

The "family coat of arms" of old identified who you were and what you stood for. If you had a coat of arms for your family today, what would it communicate about your family? Is yours a tapestry woven with the fruits of love, joy, peace, patience, and kindness? Do the threads of your spiritual heritage, passed down from generation to generation, show through?

If you were to draw a coat of arms to represent the stuff of which your family is made, what would it look like? You could start with choosing symbols for different qualities, as families used to use flowers for virtues, animals for power, and specific colors for other qualities. Make a symbol chart and then let each person contribute to the coat of arms. Or you could have each person draw their own coat of arms and then combine them into one drawing. It might make a great family Christmas card (with the symbol chart attached for clarification!).[14]

MOM READING:

60 One-Minute Family Builders, David and Claudia Arp
Adventures for Growing Families, Wes and Sheryl Haystead

Children Who Do Too Little, Patricia Sprinkle
Family Is Still a Great Idea, H. Norman Wright
Family Share Together series, Deborah Shaw Lewis and Gregg Lewis
Grandma's Little Activity Book, Margolyn Woods
Grandmother Time Again, Judy Gattis Smith
Grandparenting by Grace, Irene M. Endicott
Growing a Family Where People Really Like Each Other, Karen Dockrey
Let's Make a Memory, Shirley Dobson and Gloria Gaither
Memory Makers magazine: a magazine for the crafter of family photo
    albums; 1–800–366–6465; or P.O. Box 1929, Broomfield, CO
    80038–1929
Sing Me to Sleep and Wake Me with a Song, Helen Haidle
The Strong Family, Charles R. Swindoll
Stuff That Matters for Single Parents, Patricia Lorenz
Table Talk, Mary Beth Lagerborg and Mimi Wilson
Together at Home, Dean and Grace Merrill

LAP READING:

Evan's Corner, Elizabeth Hill
Five Minutes' Peace, Jill Murphy
The Great Alphabet Fight, Joni Eareckson Tada and Steve Jensen
I'll Fix Anthony, Judith Viorst
Mike Mulligan and His Steam Shovel, Virginia Lee Burton
Peter's Chair, Ezra Jack Keats
Spider Sisters, John Trent

Four

Discipline:
Give-Me-Limits Love

Carol turned from stirring the pot on the stove to survey the room. Jay's head was bent over his book and papers at the table. Fourth grade was tough for him; he had nearly three hours of homework every night.

Scanning over the counter, she could see baby Benjamin, swinging in his swing in the family room, his head flopped over as he slept. And here came four-year-old Scott. Again.

"Mommy, read me this book! Now, Mommy!" he demanded. Carol sighed and gathered her patience. Scott had been like this all afternoon. *Mommy* this, *Mommy* that, *Mommy* ... *Mommy*! Now, close to dinnertime, she was just hanging on. She grabbed a fistful of hamburger meat and began to shape it into a ball.

"Scott, honey, I told you that I'm busy right now. We're all hungry. I'll read the book to you at bedtime. Now, please, honey, go and play in the other room or bring your toys in here near me and play."

"No!" Scott erupted with a screech. "I want the book NOW!"

Carol saw the anger mounting in her young son's face as he yanked on her leg with all of his thirty-five pounds. Regaining her balance against his tugs, she looked down and said firmly, "Scott, I'm going to count to three and then you need to be getting your toys. One ... two ... Scott, you only have one more number.... two-and-a-half... three."

"NOOOOO!! I don't want to play with my toys! I want the book!!!!!" In what seemed to be one motion, Scott released her leg, threw the book across the room and himself on the floor at Carol's feet. He arched his back, kicked his feet, opened his mouth, and wailed. This was one pitched fit if she'd ever seen one.

Carol glanced across the room at Jay. "Gosh, Mom, what's the deal with him?" Jay asked, rolling his eyes and hunkering down over his paper.

"Oh, Jay, I've got no clue," Carol answered as she laid down the half-formed hamburger patty and searched for a towel to wipe off her greasy hands. In her mind she tried to answer some questions. What *was* going on with Scott? Was he tired? He hadn't taken a nap. Did he need more attention? She had been so busy with the baby today. Did he feel lost in the middle without his own turf? Jay had never acted like this. Maybe he was hungry. Maybe *she* was hungry. What does he want? No, what does he *need*?

All these questions whirred through her mind as they did so many times when discipline seemed the only solution. Mothering was tough sometimes. So many options ... and decisions. What was right for right now? She looked down at her child, kicking his feet on the floor, and made a quick decision: He needed limits.

She tossed the towel aside, bent down, and gathered her hefty son up from the floor, took his hand and firmly led him to his room, and shut the door behind them. Dinner could just wait a few minutes.

WHAT IS DISCIPLINE?

There are times when children simply need discipline. Their actions ask for a Give-Me-Limits Love, and nothing else will do. We discipline them because we love them, and they ask for that kind of love. Family expert Ron Hutchcraft says, "To discipline is to love. Failing to discipline is failing to love."[1] We discipline our children to prepare them for life. "Parenting with love and limits, with warmth and consequences, produces confident children who have a sense of control over their lives," write Drs. Henry Cloud and John Townsend in *Boundaries*.[2]

Discipline is training through containing. It's setting limits or boundaries with clearly defined consequences, which provides the training necessary for children to make good choices and to live life well. For us as mothers, discipline means setting limits and then carrying through with logical consequences when the boundaries or limits are overstepped.

> *My four-year-old daughter was purposely acting bad, which she does not do often. After pushing me to the limit, I disciplined her. Then she began skipping and singing around the house, hugging me and saying, "I love you, Mommy." It's as if she needed to know I cared enough about her to enforce the rules.*
>
> — ❧ —

The Purpose of Discipline

What is the purpose of setting limits for our children? Some purposes are obvious, while others are more subtle.

Protection

Babies come into this world completely helpless and dependent upon others for their very existence. As children grow, boundaries must be set to ensure their safety. Thus, we childproof our homes and require that they eat nutritionally balanced foods. We teach refusal skills and stranger awareness. And we set limits for behavior through discipline.

Think how often you apply limits for the protection of your child. You raise your voice and say, "Don't ever run out into the street without looking!" You insist, "Yes, you must buckle this safety strap if you're going to sit in the grocery cart" or "Remember, you may watch only one TV program today."

Discipline provides limits that protect our children by keeping them away from danger. As we set limits, we also give our children ample opportunities to apply what they are learning to life.

Security

Children actually want limits. Clear and consistent boundaries provide security. When a child is told that disobedience will bring a certain consequence, and then Mom follows through with that consequence, trust is built. Mom can be taken at her word. She means what she says. And that feels good to a child.

In a way, childhood is a time when children vacillate between two extremes: risk-taking and stability. To grow, they have to stretch and risk. But to be safe, they need stability. As writer and father Randolph Sanders puts it, "Children need parents to define how far is enough."[3]

Respect

I remind myself that I'm like a traffic cop. When he stops someone, he doesn't need to scream at the person, but instead he is courteous, because he's enforcing the rules and is in the right. It's the driver that is in the wrong.

— ❧ —

Further, discipline teaches respect for authority. Claudia Arp, an authority on family life, writes, "Children who do not respect their parents and other adults will have lifelong prob-

lems with authority figures."⁴ Limits actually help children develop respect for the limit-setter.

In life, we must submit ourselves to people and laws to
succeed. Teachers, police, principals, baby-sitters, parents, and
bosses have say over what is permissible and advisable behavior.
To achieve and keep peace in our society, our children need to
learn a healthy respect for those limits that make their lives make
sense.

Responsibility

In order for children to grow toward independence and
take their place as adults, they must assume various responsibilities for themselves. They must learn to handle their money, to
hold a job, and to manage emotions, to name a few. As they
grow up, they learn that freedom and responsibility go together.

Discipline is the training by which we teach our children
to accept responsibility and gain freedom. We give limits and
then give children opportunities to practice staying within those
limits. When they don't, they experience consequences. For instance, they learn to manage money if they spend their entire allowance on candy and don't have money to go to a movie with
their friends later in the week. They learn to care for living
things when, having forgotten to feed the dog, he whines at
them in the middle of the night and they need to get out of bed
to fill his dish. And they learn to manage their emotions appropriately when they can't watch TV because they threw a fit.

Training

Lastly, discipline trains a child in self-discipline and prepares
the child for his future as an adult. In fact, early and consistent
external discipline by parents provides the roots for internal self-
discipline, which brings independence. A child, given boundaries
and disciplined to learn to do his chores or homework before

Kids almost beg to know who's in charge!
Of course, they think it's them!

— ❧ —

playing, begins to form the habit of getting work done first, which leads to maturity and independence.

Richard Foster, author of *Celebration of Discipline,* defines discipline as "being able to do what needs to be done when it needs to be done." Though parents enforce that result externally in the beginning, the aim is to train the child so that he or she learns to take out the garbage or go to bed on his own when that task needs to be done.

In other words, both for behavior and emotional health, external discipline helps our children to develop internal discipline.

The Practice of Discipline

Most of us agree that children need limits, or discipline; however, many moms disagree about what discipline looks like. Or more specifically, what the appropriate consequences should be for disobedience. Three warnings. Time-out in your room. Withholding a privilege. A spanking. We will not decide that debate here. It is a debate that will continue as long as parents remain free-thinking individuals, and each family will have to decide for themselves.

When my daughter was in her terrible twos, she decided one day to have a monster tantrum. I tried to ignore her, but finally I had to discipline her. Immediately afterwards, she hugged me very intensely. She was communicating her need for the boundaries and control she did not have.

— ❧ —

Instead, let's look at the main ingredients of the practice of discipline. The first major ingredient is love. All discipline is based on love. Pediatrician Ross Campbell stresses that "making a child feel loved is the first and most important part of good discipline."[5] In disciplining your child—in setting limits and determining consequences—stop and ask yourself, are you doing this out of love?

The second main ingredient is the choice of limits, and the third, consequences. "Limits and consequences provide structure to our personality and security in the world around us," write Drs. Cloud and Townsend in *The Mom Factor*. "The good-enough mother is one who allows freedom, sets limits, and enforces the rules with consequences."[6] Guidelines for setting limits and choosing consequences are discussed later in this chapter. Moms play an important role in disciplining.

WHEN MOM'S NEEDS BUMP INTO A CHILD'S NEEDS FOR LIMITS

As we've said throughout this book, meeting the needs of our children seems to get tangled up in meeting our own needs. To know how best to meet a child's need for Give-Me-Limits

Disciplining my children is difficult for me because I hate conflict. I have to remind myself that teaching my children to mind will save them from a lot of heartache in the long run. Allowing them not to obey is cruel.

— ❧ —

Love, we're wise to take a look at our own needs. Several of them are bound to bump into a child's need for limits.

"I Want You to Like Me."

This is a big one. When our child throws a fit or begs for a new toy or disobeys an explicit rule, a tug-of-war begins in our hearts. On one hand, we know a child needs limits; on the other hand, we want our child to like us. Saying no makes a child angry and causes him to withhold love from us, at least temporarily. In such a situation, clarify your goal. Is your goal to be liked, or is it to meet your child's need? When adult children look back at their mothers, they report liking those mothers who disciplined them. In fact, they often smile and confess they are following her example. So resist the urge to give in to the heart-tug of being liked temporarily, instead of giving limits.

Know when it is more important to say no than to say yes.

The late Erma Bombeck, the consummate mother and humorist, wrote of this tug-of-war in her book *Forever Erma*. Here are a few of her thoughts, ending with the most important:

I want to be liked by my children, and it's very hard to accept when sometimes I'm not.

— ‰ —

> I loved you enough not to make excuses for your lack of respect or your bad manners.
>
> I loved you enough to accept you for what you are, not what I wanted you to be.
>
> But most of all, I loved you enough to say no when you hated me for it. That was the hardest part of all.[7]

"I Want Life to Be Easy."

This need feels familiar too. You're tired. Molly wants another cookie, and you've already said no because it will spoil her appetite for dinner. You watch her face pucker, and you give in because it's just easier. At least for now. But in the long run?

This mom-need is especially tough when we're in public. Checking out at the grocery store: "Sure, have some gum—if that will keep you quiet until we're out of here. Just don't embarrass me." Or when your husband is out of town you tell the kids: "Yes, tonight you can do anything you want to do. Even watch TV until bedtime. That will give me a few hours of peace." Or when you're on the telephone: "Yes, you can pull out all those pots and pans, even though they are off limits normally. When I'm on the phone the rules are all different because it's just easier that way."

This mom often does a child's chores for him, or even does his homework "because it's just easier that way." Drs. Cloud and Townsend name this kind of a

It is so hard to be consistent, especially when you have more than one child. Sleep deprivation makes it easy to let things go that probably shouldn't.

— ❧ —

mother in *The Mom Factor*. "The mother who finds it difficult to set boundaries with her child and to allow her to experience the consequences of her own behavior is an 'enabler.' This mother expects a certain standard of performance, but when this standard is violated she fails to enforce or allow consequences."[8]

Beware of this mom-need. You can make life more livable for yourself and your children if you look past your need for what's easier and choose what's best in the long run.

"I'm Angry!"

Watch out for this powerful need to deal with our own feelings. Our children can make us angry, especially at those moments when they need discipline. That's when a mom's need to deal with her own anger bumps into a child's need for immediate limits! But we know we should not discipline a child out of anger and frustration. While that may make us feel better, it's not good for the child. So whether or not it's convenient or easy, we need to take the time to calm down and sort through our own anger before disciplining.

Put the child in a room or playpen and take your own time-out. Separate yourself and count to ten. Give yourself time

I was not trained in discipline. It is hard to teach what I do not know myself. When my own needs are not being met, I don't take the time and effort involved to make sure theirs are.

— ❧ —

to think rationally through your limit-making and consequences. Cool down and then express your feelings in appropriate words. Go on to set limits and consequences. As legitimate as your own emotions may be, they can skew the limits you are working to set. And emotions are powerful. If you are truly worried about your ability to control your anger in dealing with your child, seek help. It's the best thing you can do for both of you.

Mom-needs are always legitimate. They must be recognized, understood, and carefully responded to, especially as we work to meet our child's need for limits. Too often the following words of family expert Ron Hutchcraft ring true. "Discipline is to teach; punishment is to unload anger. Discipline is reasoned; punishment is inflamed emotion. Discipline is thought through; punishment is too enraged to think. When parents discipline, they are working on their child's needs, but when they simply punish, parents are working mostly on their own needs."[9]

GUIDELINES FOR DISCIPLINE

Are you ready now for some help in giving Give-Me-Limits Love? Here goes!

Set Few Rules and Tie Them to Real Consequences

Two points are important here. Let's take them one at a time.

Set few rules

Children need and appreciate rules that are consistently enforced, so be intentional about setting rules. Limit the number of rules and choose your battles carefully, because children are confused by too many rules. Keep rules clear, concise, and consistent. Agree with your husband about what the rules should

When I discipline, whether it's a time-out or a spanking or something else, I call my child back to me, hold him, say "I love you," and then go over why he was disciplined. This way love and learning are taking place.

— ❧ —

be. Speak of them ahead of time. Make the boundaries age-appropriate, reasonable, and measurable, when possible. Set rules your child is capable of keeping. For instance, do not set rules about using the toilet when a toddler is not yet able to achieve success in potty training.

Communicate the agreed-upon rules to the child and ask him to repeat them back to you, so you know the rules are heard. And then remind your child of the rules again and again as they come into real-life applications. "We always sit at the table when we eat." "We only watch an hour of TV each day."

A younger child will have more rules than an older child. The idea is to start with stricter control and move toward fewer rules and greater freedom as the child grows up. Pediatrician Grace Ketterman illustrates limit-setting with the image of enlarging the enclosure of a young colt. "As he grows, his fences must be pushed back, or he will break them down."[10]

Instead of always setting rules with a preschooler, consider offering choices, with all the options being acceptable to you. "Do you want a bagel or cereal before you go out to play?" You undermine the growing confidence of a child if you offer a choice and then disagree with the child's decision. Offering choices is a way to allow children to take ownership of the desire to stay within the limits, while encouraging them toward your goals.

Tie rules to real consequences

One of the best lessons we can teach our children is that life is full of "if . . . then" scenarios. We train them for life by teaching them about natural consequences. Certain behavior brings certain consequences. If she throws a fit, then she will have a time-out. If he hits his little sister, he will not watch his favorite program on television tonight. If she doesn't do her chores, she can't play on the computer.

In their parenting curriculum, *Success in Parenting*, Drs. Foster Cline and Benjamin Brucker outline two kinds of consequences: natural and imposed.[11] Natural consequences happen naturally as a result of certain behaviors. When we're polite and friendly, people like us. When we get angry or nasty, people pull away. When we consume the whole bag of candy, we get a stomachache. When we hit someone, we may get hit back. When we stay up too late, we have trouble getting up in the morning. Natural consequences motivate our children in the right direction as they are rewarded for good behavior and given discomfort for problem behavior.

Sometimes it is hard to give discipline because it makes your children cry and you feel guilty. But my mom always quoted the saying, "Either they cry now or you will cry later," meaning that the problems will only get worse along with the consequences for children raised without discipline.

— ❧ —

Cline and Brucker note that imposed consequences are set as a result of certain behaviors, usually problem behaviors. They are set ahead of time and consistently enforced in order to train a child and derive their best effect. "When you hit your sister, you have to go to your room." "When you throw a tantrum in the grocery store, we will leave and go right to the car and you will be punished."

Parents should be intentional about setting consequences. Determine them ahead of time, free from the crisis of misbehavior. Remember that consequences help the child learn to choose the right behavior for his own benefit. Consequences should be age-appropriate, logical, and reasonable, which means fitting the seriousness of the infraction. Once determined, consequences should be clearly stated to the child.

Once this process is in place, we should stand back and allow a child to experience the consequences of her behavior, rather than get in the way and protect that child from those consequences. When we rescue or overprotect a child from logical consequences of behavior, we rob that child of the opportunity to learn a critical coping skill for life.

Distinguish Between "By Accident" and "On Purpose" in Disobedience

Recognize the difference between "by accident" and "on purpose" in responding to your child's disobedience. Pediatrician and child-psychologist James Dobson calls this "childish irresponsibility" versus "willful disobedience." Once labeled, you can handle the situation appropriately.

For example, a child reaches for his milk and knocks it over. This is "by accident" and should be handled with patience and a wad of paper towels. However, jumping on his chair and crashing into his milk after being told to sit properly in his chair might be considered an "on purpose" behavior and the child should be disciplined, not for the spilled milk but for refusing to sit down in his chair.

Delayed Gratification— Teach Your Child that Waiting is Part of Life

Much satisfaction and contentment in life is based on the ability to wait. Or to put first things first. Or to be able to say no to something we want right now to get something better in the future. This is called "delayed gratification," and it is an important coping skill. When we are consistent in meeting a child's needs early in life, we help that child learn about delayed gratification because she trusts that her needs will, indeed, be met. When we consistently meet a baby's needs, that child begins to learn we are trustworthy and begins to learn to delay gratification by the end of the first year.

How can we use discipline to meet this need? When a year-old baby cries to be fed and sees you starting the process to get his food, you can tell him to be quiet because food is coming. He learns that his needs are being met, and he can wait. An older child likes to have some money of his own to spend. Instead of always giving cash and then taking a youngster to the store to spend it, encourage your child to save his allowance for something he wants to buy and then take him, fistful of change and all, to make the purchase.

I have started keeping a list of disciplines that have been assigned so that I keep to my word and don't forget to follow through (trash duty for the week, set table for the week, no cartoons next week, etc.). We try to assign chores relating to whatever caused the problem.

— ❧ —

Instruct your children to listen to each family member at the dinner table and to wait their turn to talk. Teach them to make their beds when they get up, to take their dishes from the table to the counter, to feed the cat before playing a game. These daily rituals can underline the rule that work comes before play and helps drive home the concept of delayed gratification.

Turn the Key of Consistency in Your Child's Life

When we threaten to enforce specific consequences and then fail to follow through, we only confuse our children. When we break our own policies and are exempt from our own infractions, we erode their trust in us and in the limits we've set.

Consistency is a key to Give-Me-Limits Love, and we must learn to turn it in the lives of our children. But consistency is not the same thing as perfection. Dr. Grace Ketterman re-

I have to be careful not to make too many rules on things that will not matter next year or ten years down the road. I must choose what is important enough to have consequences and then be consistent with those things.

— ❧ —

minds us that "many mothers think consistency means being totally patient, kind, and soft-spoken no matter what the situation. . . . Not only is such a maternal response inadvisable, it is also impossible!"[12] Consistency means following through, as best we can, with the understanding that sometimes we can't. Or don't. And when we don't, we're honest with our children about admitting our own mistakes. Then we start all over again.

GETTING TO THE HEART OF GIVE-ME-LIMITS LOVE

So often, when we think of loving our children and meeting their needs, we think of demonstrations of love, such as hugs and kisses. But discipline is an equally important demonstration of love. Our children need limits, and discipline is the means by which we train them to respond to those limits. It is the means by which we lovingly prepare them for the future and the self-discipline that will enable them to cope with confidence as they grow up.

Love Handles

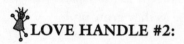**LOVE HANDLE #1:**

Guidelines for First Discipline

1. Love your baby and give lots of cuddles, hugs, smiles, and touch. The more you are around, interested and pleased, the better.
2. Give your baby lots of freedom to explore and crawl around.
3. Baby-proof your home and encourage correct behavior so that you need to say no as seldom as possible.
4. Use as few commands as possible. Use other techniques like moving the baby, moving the object, or doing what needs to be done without comment (i.e., dress the baby without comment when he fights being dressed).
5. Never say no unless the child is old enough to understand. Never say no unless you can arrange or ensure that the baby will stop doing what he is doing, either by removing the baby or removing the object.[13]

LOVE HANDLE #2:

Age-Appropriate Boundaries for Children
Birth to five months

Setting limits is not as much an issue as providing security for the infant. The only real boundary is the soothing presence of the mother. The mother's job is to help her newborn contain intense, frightening, and conflicting feelings. The screaming four-month-old is trying to find out whether the world is a reasonably safe place. Teaching delay of gratification shouldn't begin until after the first year of life, when a foundation of safety has been established between baby and mother. Just as grace always precedes truth (John 1:17), attachment must come before separation.

Five to ten months

Children are learning "Mother and I aren't the same" and are beginning to move toward the scary, fascinating world out there. To help children develop good boundaries in this stage, parents need to encourage attempts at separateness while still being the anchors to which the child clings. At this point, most infants don't have the ability to understand and respond appropriately to the word no. Keeping them out of danger by picking them up and removing them from unsafe places is the best route.

Ten to eighteen months

A baby now has the emotional and cognitive ability to understand and respond to the word no. Boundaries become increasingly important, both having and hearing limits. Allowing the child's "no muscle" to develop is crucial at this age. Saying no is your child's way of finding out whether taking responsibility for her life has good results or whether saying no causes someone to withdraw. Help your child see that she is not the center of the universe and that there are consequences for scribbling on doors or screaming in church.

Eighteen to thirty-six months

The child is now learning to take responsibility for a separate yet connected soul who realizes life has limits. To teach a child boundaries at this stage, you need to respect her no whenever appropriate, yet maintain your own firm no. Pick your battles carefully and choose important ones to win. The child can learn the rules now, as well as the consequences for breaking them. Here's a suggested process:

1. First infraction: Tell the child not to color on the bedsheet and help the child meet her need to color in another way, such as using a coloring book.
2. Second infraction: Again tell the child no and state the consequence—she will take a time-out or lose the crayons for the rest of the day.
3. Third infraction: Administer the consequences, explaining why, then give the child a few minutes to feel angry and separate from you.
4. Comfort and reconnection: Hold and comfort the child, which helps her reattach with you and helps her differentiate between consequences and a loss of love.[14]

LOVE HANDLE #3:

Saying No to Your Baby

When is a baby able to take no for an answer? Although almost all parents are able to discern when their children understand the meaning of no, this ability generally develops throughout the second twelve months. During this time, the child learns about autonomy and the response to authority. Some basic rules can guide you in the manner you tell your baby no.

Baby "No" Rule #1: Never tell your baby what to do before your baby can understand you or is able to do what you want done.

Baby "No" Rule #2: Do not say no more than absolutely necessary.

Baby "No" Rule #3: Only say no when you have control of the situation.

Note: When the parent tells a baby no, the baby sometimes hesitates, looks slyly at the parent, and then does
the forbidden action, as if to say impishly, "Now what
are you going to do?" Some parents think this type of
noncompliance is cute. It is a little bit cute in an infant.
It's not cute in a six- or seven-year old.[15]

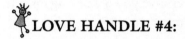

LOVE HANDLE #4:

Six Keys to Shaping a Child's Will

1. Define the boundaries before they are enforced.
2. When defiantly challenged, respond with confident de-
   cisiveness.
3. Distinguish between willful defiance and childish irresponsibility.
4. Reassure and teach after the confrontation is over.
5. Avoid impossible demands.
6. Let love be your guide![16]

LOVE HANDLE #5:

Ten Rules for the Terrible Twos

1. Challenge him to explore, play, and be constructively
   creative. Be the guide.
2. When she whines and acts babyish, don't scold or tell
   her to grow up. Give her some babying. She has no
   better way to let you know she needs just that.
3. Spend more time and energy finding activities he can
   do and less telling him, "Stop!"
4. Keep your rules few and simple, focused on structuring
   your child's days. Enforce them firmly and kindly and
   consistently.

5. Give only simple choices, but allow your child to make some decisions.

6. Avoid dishonesty. Threats you will not enforce or questions for which you already have the answers are dishonest. Never ask, "Don't you want to put away your toys now and take a nap?" No self-respecting toddler will say, "Of course, Mommy!" And don't say, "If you tip over your glass, I'll never give you a drink again!" It may be tempting, but it's not true.

7. When your child throws a tantrum, don't react with an even bigger one. Simply take charge. Hold your child firmly and lovingly until he regains control.

8. Watch your child frequently. When she starts getting frustrated at play or shows fatigue, go to her and help her over the hump or put her down for a nap. Don't help so much that she believes she can do nothing without you, however.

9. Plan for her seesaw life. Challenge her to be even more independent than she demands when she is in that mode. With equal sincerity, cuddle, rock, and baby her when she reverts to needing to be little for a while.

10. Capture the child's curiosity, and use it to encourage exploring, learning, and sharing adventure.[17]

LOVE HANDLE #6:

How to Use Time-Outs

Time-outs are especially useful with preschoolers who have problems with blatant disobedience. You may want to use a kitchen timer or the timer on your microwave. Set it for a predetermined amount of time, usually one minute for each year of the child's age. The child should be placed in a chair away from family activity, maybe in another room (but not their bedroom). When the child is sitting quietly, the time begins.

When the bell goes off, ask the child what he or she did wrong. Assure the child of your love and acceptance with a positive statement, such as, "I love you, but you must not do that again." Then give the child a hug.[18]

LOVE HANDLE #7:

Dealing with Tantrums

Q: My four-year-old breaks into a crying fit whenever I say no. It can be no to a snack before supper or no to going to play at a friend's house or anything else she doesn't like.

A: For several days, keep track of when the tantrums happen. Tantrums often occur when a child has not received adequate warning of a change about to happen. She's tired or hungry or hasn't had a hug or attention from you for a while. Add this new information to what you already know about your child. For example, perhaps she is especially cranky right after she gets up in the morning. Because you are the expert on your child, you know the morning routines go more smoothly if she eats first. Or, you know that your child needs time for transitions. For example, tell your child that lunch will be in ten minutes, so he can finish what he is doing.

As you seek to eliminate opportunities for tantrums, be consistent in your response. When your child throws a tantrum, simply walk away. Do this every single time, as long as she can't hurt herself or someone else. Some children act up simply to get attention.[19]

LOVE HANDLE #8:

Clear Messages

Parents sometimes confuse their children with mixed messages instead of using clear, direct messages. Here are a few examples:

- The Tease: When parents say "We'll see" or "I'll think about it" when they really mean no, they are practicing the "tease." Teasers avoid confrontation but raise a child's hopes, making the inevitable confrontation worse. The remedy: If no is the answer, say it.
- The Wheedle: Asking your children to do something instead of putting your wishes into a clear statement is *wheedling*. For example: "I sure would appreciate some help bringing in the groceries." The remedy: Use simple, direct instructions. "I need help with the groceries. Now."
- The Shuttle: When neither parent wants to take responsibility for a decision, they'll bounce the youngster back and forth between them. Shuttling is an attempt to avoid a confrontation with the child, but it increases the odds of confrontation and teaches a child how to be manipulative. The remedy: Say yes or no or "I'll talk to your father, and we'll let you know."[20]

LOVE HANDLE #9:

Differences Between Consequences and Punishment

1. Punishment attempts to make the child feel bad.

Consequences help the situation or decrease the hassle to others.

2. Punishment is usually done in anger.
   Consequences are usually done with understanding and empathy.

3. With punishment, the child ends up resentful.
   With consequences, the child more likely ends up thoughtful.

4. When angry parents punish, the punishment may have nothing to do with the infraction.
   Consequences should fit the infraction.[21]

LOVE HANDLE #10:

Learning Rules, Family Style

Here are some suggestions to help you help your children learn about rules in a family setting.

1. Have a family meeting and discuss your family's rules. Ask, "Why is it important to obey these rules?" If you need to establish some new rules, enlist everyone's help in deciding what is fair.

2. Discuss a game that you all enjoy and talk about the rules of the game. Why is it important to have rules in a game?

3. Take some time to look at the Ten Commandments in the Bible (Ex. 20:1–17). Talk about the possible reasons God had for giving these commandments and asking his people to obey them.

4. Discuss a current event or newspaper article that shows the consequences of disobedience.[22]

LOVE HANDLE #11:

Take Care of Yourself, Mom

"There are occasions in the life of every mother when she looks in the mirror and asks, 'How can I make it through this day?'" Here's a suggestion. Dr. James Dobson counsels, "Reserve some time for yourself. It is important for a mother to put herself on the priority list, too. At least once a week she should play tennis, go bowling or shopping, stop by the gym, or simply 'waste' an occasional afternoon. It is unhealthy for anyone to work all the time."[23]

MOM READING:

Boundaries and Kids, Dr. Henry Cloud and Dr. John Townsend
    (available Spring 1998)
How to Live with Your Parents Without Losing Your Mind, Ken Davis
Making Children Mind Without Losing Yours, Kevin Leman
The New Dare to Discipline, James Dobson
The Strong-Willed Child, James Dobson
Success in Parenting (curriculum), Foster Cline and Ben Brucker
When You Feel Like Screaming, Grace Ketterman and Pat Holt

LAP READING:

Bedtime for Frances (and other *Frances* books), Russell Hoban
The Berenstain Bears Forget Their Manners, Stan and Jan Berenstain
The Berenstain Bears Get the Gimmes, Stan and Jan Berenstain
The Big Hungry Bear, Audrey Wood
The Christopher Churchmouse Treasury, Barbara Davoll
The Little Engine that Could, Watty Piper

Five

Guidance:
Show-Me-and-Tell-Me Love

Whew!" Brenda said under her breath as she finally pushed her full cart into line at the checkout counter. She adjusted baby Trevor's seatbelt and looked around for four-year-old Hillary. There she was, a few feet in front of her, studying the candy display conveniently located just at her eye level. "Why do stores put those temptations right there?" Brenda wondered as she reached for Hillary's hand and guided her into the line next to their cart. The lady in front of them was putting away her wallet. Good. It was their turn.

"Hi there, Sweet-kins!" the checker winked at Hillary from her height over the counter and then smiled at Brenda. Returning her gaze to Hillary, she asked, "Where did you get all that gorgeous blonde hair? My, my, you look like an indoor ray of sunshine!" Hillary's eyes widened as she listened. "And look at that precious teddy bear you've got! What's his name? Or is he a she? I bet that bear is pretty special to you. You've nearly rubbed all the fur off around his ears and—look—he's even lost an eye! Yes, ma'am. He must be one loved bear! What did you say his name was?"

The checker chatted on, rosy cheeks glowing, chin wagging in a comfortable way, her hands moving expertly as she scanned one item after another, never missing a price code. She was doing her thing.

Hillary, on the other hand, had wrapped both arms around Brenda's leg as if it were a tree trunk and she was in the middle of a windstorm. Head back, chin up, her eyes searched Brenda's with uncertainty.

Brenda quickly took in her ambivalence. As if she could read her mind, Brenda heard the simultaneous questions forming, "Mommy! She's a stranger! Should I talk to a stranger?" and "Mommy! She's being friendly. Should I be friendly back?" Important questions that needed answers—and demanded choices.

So many lessons to teach a child! First, it's okay to touch the water because it's fun and helps us clean our hands. Then, it's be careful because the water might be hot. First, it's encouragement to use a voice freely as speech is discovered. Then, it's the difference between a soft voice and a hard voice. First, it's don't walk in the street! Then, it's look both ways before you cross. So much to teach. So many layers and choices. And for most of the teaching it is up to moms to be the guide.

Brenda reached down and patted her daughter on the head. "It's okay to talk to strangers as long as Mommy or Daddy is with you," she told her softly as the checker spoke to someone else over her shoulder. Then Brenda lifted Hillary up to the checker's eye level. "Can you tell the nice lady what you named your bear?"

Hillary smiled and announced, "Bunny! My bear's name is Bunny!" Now relaxing in her mother's arms, Hillary once again became her confident, outgoing self.

As Brenda put her down and fumbled for her checkbook, she considered the impact of that moment. "I don't know what to do or how to do it, Mommy. I need you to show me and tell me," Hillary had seemed to say. Brenda was glad she'd read the signals and made it through one more mothering moment.

GUIDE MY WAY

Children's questions. They start out simple at first. What color is the car?" or "Who is my Grandma?" Then they get a bit more difficult. "Why does Daddy have a beard and you don't?" and "Why do dogs have four legs instead of two?" Finally, they get deeper and more challenging because they involve choices. "Do I always have to tell the truth?" "What if I don't like someone?" "Should I ever talk to strangers?"

Children aren't born knowing the answers or knowing what to do when. They need guidance that includes knowing what to do, how to do it, and when to do it.

Sometimes my child asks questions when he knows the answer, so I think he just wants to confirm his knowledge. When he hears the answer, he says to himself, "Yeah, that's what I thought!"

— ❧ —

They need a Show-Me-and-Tell-Me Love that demonstrates and models as it teaches about life.

A Mother's Guidance

Who better to offer a living illustration—to guide a child through a laboratory experiment of trial and error—than Mom, who lives day in and day out, both with and before her little ones? She is like a canine companion to the blind, leading the way, interpreting signals, providing information, showing the consequences for wrong choices, all with the goal of guiding the learner. "Show me and tell me, Mommy. I need you to help me find my way."

When Mom Is Unsure of Her Way

Okay. So we're supposed to be able to meet this need for guidance in our child. But sometimes we're not sure we can!

"But I don't even know my way.
How can I show the way to my child?"

A mom needs to be aware of her own strengths and weaknesses and handle herself accordingly. Then she can help her children gain self-awareness.

— ❧ —

The thought of being a guide to a child is more than some moms can fathom. We still feel like children ourselves! Hey—we're still trying to figure out what we want to be when *we* grow up!

The great news is that moms can learn *with* their children. Becoming a mother defines our identity and our future, but only as a kind of backdrop for life. Within the context of mothering, we still have many, many choices to make. Life is a process of discovery that we can share with our children.

"What about when I don't know the answers?"

All day long—and all night long—come the questions. How are we supposed to know all the answers? A huge part inside of us just wants to put our head in the sand and ignore our children's need for guidance. *They'll figure it out,* we think. We've made too many mistakes in the past to qualify as teachers today.

Once again, relax. Moms don't have to have all the answers. They just need to know where to get them. Acquaint yourself with your pediatrician. Get to know your child's teachers. Pick up a book on discipline. Gather information and make some choices that are appropriate for your child. That's how you fill in the blanks for yourself.

"How can I be a model to my child
when I do it wrong myself?"

So many times we blow it as moms. We lose our tempers. A naughty word escapes from our mouths. We greedily refuse to share our doughnut (okay, that's just because it's the first one we've had to ourselves in months). How can we be models to our children when we do so much wrong ourselves? They ought to look at us and learn what *not* to do!

The book *Mom to Mom* answers this question honestly for us. "We teach our children to live life well by modeling life-living before them, including our triumphs, failures, and apologies.

Being a mom requires such patience and self-control. My first response is to screech, but I can't teach my children patience and self-control if I'm are reacting without those qualities!

— 🐝 —

What more could a child ask for in a laboratory experience of how to live life?"[1] We don't have to be perfect to be good models before our children. If we were, we would just set up an unrealistic standard for our children. They can't be perfect either!

MOTIVATING THE MIND OF A CHILD

How do we meet our child's need for Show-Me-and-Tell-Me Love? How do we effectively offer the guidance needed? We start by considering what goes on in the mind of a child, what motivates a child to learn. A child's mind is made up of many mysterious and miraculous components that help her to learn. As moms, we tap into the motivators of imagination, curiosity, and creativity as we guide. There are other components as well.

In *The Key to Your Child's Heart,* Gary Smalley identifies a child's unique or particular bent as the greatest motivation for learning. Parents successfully guide young learners when they identify these bents, tracking their children's interests and desires and encouraging them to pursue their unique, God-given potential. Smalley lists some specific techniques that can be used to motivate a child as you identify these bents:

1. Help children choose their own goals.
2. Help children visualize the positive results of achieving their own goals and the negative results of not reaching their goals.
3. Remember the power of praise.
4. Expose children to a variety of activities.
5. Expect children to do things right.
6. Believe your children can achieve great things.
7. Help children develop a more positive self-image.
8. Reward your children.
9. Use the ol' "You can do it, can't you?" principle.
10. Expose your children to people you admire.
11. Be persistent.
12. Be enthusiastic.
13. Develop strong inner convictions.[2]

We meet our children's needs for Show-Me-and-Tell-Me Love and maximize the guidance we offer when we tap into the foundational motivators of their minds.

THE CONTENT OF SHOW-ME-AND-TELL-ME LOVE

We also maximize our guidance by determining what we ourselves value. What are the messages we want to give our children through our guidance? To get us thinking about the answer, we can turn to moms who have raised their children. What messages did they pass on or wish they had passed on?

When songwriter Gloria Gaither, now a grandmother, sat down to consider what she would give her children if she had mothering to do again, among other things she decided she would give them "the gift of solitude, the gift of knowing the joy of silence, the chance to be alone and not feel uncomfortable . . . I would teach our children to cry . . . to sense the empti-ness of the deserted . . . to understand the hopelessness of the powerless. . . . Last, I would teach our children to soar, to rise above the common and yet find delight in the commonplace, to fly over the distracting disturbances of life yet see from this per-spective ways to attack knotty problems that can thwart growth and stymie development."[3]

When our children are young, they are dependent upon us for guidance. They look to us for teaching about everything from the everyday struggles of how to tie their shoes to how to define their identities, make hard choices, and live out their lives. If we want to raise children whose needs for guidance are met, we must first determine what we ourselves value and want to integrate into their personalities. Then we intentionally guide them toward these qualities. Show-Me-and-Tell-Me Love offers guidance in three basic categories.

Character

What does your family believe in? Chil-dren unconsciously seek out our philosophy of life, what we stand for, believe in, what is at the core of our beings. If it is strong philosophy, we model it by the decisions we make. Values like hon-esty, patience, kindness, love, equality, freedom, service, and integrity are communicated in the choices we make every day. Character is produced by the way we model those values

As an older mom, I encourage new moms to learn to love themselves and to express their God-given talents joyfully. When you are comfortable and secure in yourself, it is much easier to transfer a sense of secu-rity and genuine love to others. This em-powers children to be independent and happy as well. Children are like little barometers—they are very sensitive to the conditions around them.

— ❧ —

and pass messages about them on to our children. Here are some ways to help you intentionally consider your values.

Identify what you value

List ten values you would like to see in your children. Look at the suggestions in the preceding paragraph for starters. Work to make your own list positive rather than negative. For example, consider what you are "for"—not what you are "against." Positive values are much more attractive to children than negative ones. When good things are planted in hearts, evil things are displaced. The best starting place for passing on our values is identifying them for ourselves.

Reexamine your own character

It's been said that character is who you are in the dark. Or, character is who you are when nobody is watching. Children are always watching. Take a tough look at who you are—all the time. Do you say you value respect for authority but get angry if a policeman stops you for going five miles over the speed limit? Do you value honesty but pay for one trip through the salad bar and get enough for everyone at your table?

Be the example of who you want your children to be. When you see them trying on your high heels and clomping around the house, know that the shoes are not all they are trying on. They are also trying on your attitudes, your reactions to things, your habits, and your beliefs. Decide which ones you want them to wear.

— ❧ —

What traits are you proud of and which would you rather not think about? If you do an honest inventory of your own character, you're less apt to pass along some subtle messages that you don't want to communicate.

Character is a trait that is more readily caught than taught. In order to offer your child a chance at forming character of distinction, identify your own values and character.

Critical Thinking

The ability to make good choices is vital for living life well. If you want your child to live out the values and character your family establishes, train him to use critical thinking skills. These skills will move your child through the maze of life's choices with confidence and success.

Sue Lockwood Summers, an author and expert in Media Literacy Training, encourages children to think critically. She describes a continuum of thinkers, with "sponges" on one end and "cynics" on the other. "Sponges" absorb everything they see, hear, or read and assume it is all true. "Cynics" dismiss everything they see, hear, or read and assume it is all incorrect. What children need is to land somewhere in the middle of these two opposites, by developing the ability to sort through information and become a "healthy skeptic." A child needs the "skills to judge the reliability of the sources of the information, to verify the validity of the facts, and finally to reflect on the meaning and impact on his personal life."[4] Such skills must be learned and practiced over a period of time. (See the suggestions in the "Love Handles" at the end of this chapter.)

Think of the applications of such critical thinking skills in a child's everyday circumstances! Television viewing. (The average American child, before entering first grade, watches more than five thousand hours of television, more than one-fourth of his waking time.)[5] Music selection. Processing information offered in school, whether in preschool, elementary years, high school or postgraduate. Games played. Purchases made. Friends pursued. Dating, marriage, and quality of marriage. When we teach our children to think critically, sliding choices through a grid based on values and character, we give them a tool for living life well.

Life Skills

A child also needs guidance in learning basic life skills. As moms, we identify these skills and then intentionally offer guidance. Here are some suggested life skills.

Sharing

One of the battlegrounds of toddlerhood is the terrain of "sharing." Someone whose identity has remained anonymous penned a poem to express the toddler's point on the subject. It's called, appropriately, "The Toddler's Creed."

> If I want it, it's mine.
> If I give it to you and change my mind later, it's mine.
> If I can take it away from you, it's mine.
> If it's mine, it will never belong to anyone else, no matter what.
> If we are building something together, all the pieces are mine.
> If it looks just like mine, it is mine.[6]

We offer effective guidance about sharing when we consider the developmental task behind such intense ownership. Child development experts explain that in order for a child to "share" something, he must first understand that he "owns" it. Just as a child cannot develop security until he completes the task of object permanence (understanding that something is still in existence even though it has left the room and is out of sight, like Mother), so a child cannot give up a toy to another child until he understands fully that it belongs to him. Think about it. How could you loan your car to a friend if you weren't sure it was really yours? As a mom you can help a child understand ownership and sharing with this kind of suggestion: "When you are through playing with that toy, Sam, would you let Benjamin have a turn playing with it?"

Manners

It's been said that rudeness is not a lack of manners, but a lack of love, because love is not rude. Historically, the concept of etiquette began when a person was given a ticket to meet royalty. On this ticket, certain guidelines defined expected behavior. Even the youngest of children can begin to learn the guidelines of expected behavior. They can also learn that we show our love for others by using good manners. Having good manners serves a child well through his growing years.

Here are some basic suggestions that will help guide your child toward good manners:

- Emphasize the positive. Catch your child doing something right and praise him immediately. "I heard you say 'please' and 'thank you' to your grandmother. That was good."
- Be specific with your guidelines. Don't simply say, "We need to be polite when we answer the telephone." Say, "We need to say hello clearly. Then listen carefully and and tell the person that you will get your mother."
- Be patient with your child's mistakes. Children learn by making mistakes. Correct them gently but consistently. "When we eat, we chew with our mouths closed."
- Practice manners before big events. Remind your child what is expected of them. Role play with your child. "Okay, pretend that I am your grandmother at Thanksgiving dinner and I ask you what you are thankful for this year. How do you answer me?" Or, "If you want some more mashed potatoes, how do you ask for them?" Or, "When you are introduced to Mr. Smith, what do you say?"
- When your child forgets some manners, remind her by asking questions. "What is the first thing we say when we answer the telephone?" "When we talk to someone, do we look at our feet or the person's face?"

- Set a good example. Answer the telephone in the same manner you expect your child to answer the telephone. Say "please" and "thank you" when talking to your child.

Refusal skills

Outline for your children appropriate boundaries for their protection and safety. In an age-appropriate technique, teach your child how to handle strangers, what to do if she is ever separated from you in public, appropriate and inappropriate touching, phone- and door-answering skills, and then go over these matters every several months for emphasis. Use the "what-if" game for teaching. "What if we got separated?" Understanding will come at various stages.

It is vital that we not only teach these skills, but that we encourage their integration into the lives of our little ones. We thwart their ability to take care of themselves when we tell them, "Let Uncle Harry (or Aunt Bessie) kiss you!" We need to honor their comfort levels with this kind of touching. Be consistent and praise your child when she uses the skills she is learning.

Dealing with feelings

Children need guidance in learning how to handle their feelings. Is it okay to feel angry? What do I do with my angry feelings? What do I do when I feel sad? In *The Mom Factor*, Drs. Henry Cloud and John Townsend describe the special role that mothers have in helping children learn to handle their feelings. "A mother can help by talking about feelings *as feelings*. She can help her child see that feelings are something we have, not are. It's immensely helpful when mother can give a child an emotional vocabulary, such as, 'It sounds as though you're scared.' (Or angry or sad.) This does several things for the child. She now has words for those deep mysterious emotions, which, in turn, gives her a little control over them. She can now discuss them."[7]

In learning how to handle feelings, a child needs to know that it is normal to have feelings, and that feelings are not the problem, but only the symptom of a problem. According to Cloud and Townsend, "a mother can teach her child that emotions are not an enemy but a friend by helping the child set limits, confront wrongdoing in others, and know when to get out of danger."[8] The mother can give specific guidelines in dealing with feelings, such as "It's okay to feel mad at your sister and talk to her about why you are mad, but it is not okay to hit her when you feel mad."

My ten-year-old son cried, "Mom! The little boys messed up my room again and dumped out my Legos while I was at school! You promised that they weren't allowed in there!" I had let the younger boys go into the room because I had some women friends pop by and it kept the boys quiet the whole time, but I was wrong. And my son was right to express his feelings.

— ❧ —

Money

Children need guidance in knowing how to save and how to spend money. Certainly children absorb an attitude about how to save and spend from watching their parents. Many families use an allowance starting at about age five to teach children how to save and spend money. Moms can also take advantage of everyday activities to teach children about budgets and spending. For instance, in choosing between two similar products, talk about the difference in cost and quality. In general, discussions about money involve other issues, such as family values and decision-making. All these issues work together to guide children into learning the responsible use of money.

A WINNING COMBINATION: SHOW-AND-TELL

Teachers of young children know about the value of show-and-tell. The combination of sight and sound offers a powerful learning experience.

Show-Me Love

Years ago, Melicint Margaret Trimble wrote a poem on the importance of parental modeling entitled "Someone's Following Us." Though the language is a bit dated, her point is well made.

> Two little feet to follow us where e're our feet may trod.
> Will they lead to folly's trod, will they lead to God?
> Two little eyes to observe what we do, to copy our ways
>   and our tastes.
> Will they help build a growing world, or will they add to
>   the waste?
> Two little ears to hear what we say, in pleasure, in suffer-
>   ing, in prayer.
> Will it give courage and peace on the way or multiply ha-
>   tred and care?
> One little mind but two little lips, to share our thoughts
>   and words.
> Will they be envious, selfish and proud, or inculcate faith
>   in our Lord?
> One little heart but two little arms, embracing those he
>   loves;
> Tenderly, Jesus, help us direct his affection to God alone.
> Daddy and Mommy—they're magical words, secure in
>   loving trust,
> God grant us the grace to follow you Lord, for a little
>   one's following us.[9]

When we think carefully about who has most deeply impacted our lives growing up, it is most often people whose example we watched and admired, not necessarily those who said this or that. As the sayings go, "Actions speak louder than words" and "It's who you are, not what you say."

Sybil Waldrop writes,

If you are courteous, considerate and respectful, your
    child learns to be kind.
If you are generous, caring and thoughtful, your child
    learns to be giving.
If you are attentive to his needs, he becomes thoughtful
    of others.
If you are kind-spoken and loving, he learns to be gentle.
If you notice his attempts to succeed and cheer him on,
    he becomes self-confident.
If you're loud, angry and easily upset, he becomes hostile
    and irritable.
If you value your work, he learns to feel worthwhile.
If you are godlike, your child learns to love God.
If you love your child unconditionally, your child learns
    to love as God does.[10]

What will you specifically model to your children? As a
mother, will you model self-care so that your daughter learns that
moms have needs too and will embrace her own needs when she
is a mother? Will you
model strength to your
son, standing up for your
beliefs and your opinions?
Will you demonstrate
how to handle negative
feelings, how to apolo-
gize after an offense, how
to go on after a mistake,
how to respond when no
answers to prayer come,
how to accept and love

*I recently went ballistic with a mom-sized
tantrum, due to getting three kids fed,
dressed, and into the car to drive to the
school-bus stop for the umpteenth morning
in a row. I got into the car, banged my
knee, uttered something dramatic, and
was stopped cold by the looks on all three
kids' faces. It was then that I realized that
if I can't control my emotions, then how
can I expect them to have self-control?*

— ❧ —

yourself unconditionally as God does, how to survive when life has
dealt you disaster?

Tell-Me Love

In addition to showing them love, children need words.
Obviously, our words convey greater meaning when the messages behind them are modeled consistently. When our actions
model our values and beliefs, and when we use words to back
up our actions, we are using a meaningful combination to offer
guidance to our children. Here are some ways to use words in
the process of guidance.

Answer their questions

In his book *If I Were Starting My Family Again*, John
Drescher confesses, "In listening I would pay more careful attention to my child's questions. It is estimated that the average
child asks 500,000 questions by the age of fifteen. What a privilege for parents! A half million opportunities to share something about the meaning of life."[11]

The role of "Answer Mom" is one of high influence. It
takes great patience to grit your teeth and answer the gazillionth
"Why?" of the day. But believe it or not, there will come a day
when your opinion will neither be sought nor carry the weight
it does today. Answer while you can.

Tell children what they can do instead of what they can't do

Focus on the dos and avoid the don'ts. Such a practice encourages further exploration and learning rather than putting a
lid on it. Instead of saying, "Don't leave your coat on the floor,"
say, "Hang your coat up." Rather than, "Don't stand on the
couch," say, "Couches are for sitting, not standing." Instead of
saying, "Don't drag your coat in the mud," say, "Tie your coat
around your waist like this."

Whenever possible, offer choices

Critical thinking takes practice, practice, and practice, and it is never too early to start. When we offer our children choices, we demonstrate our confidence in their ability to make a decision, and we strengthen their thinking skills. A word of caution here. Wide-open choices may lead to confusion or even consequences you don't value. Try, "It's cold outside today. Would you like to wear your sweater or your jacket?" instead of, "Do you want your coat?"

Look for "teachable moments"

A child is most motivated to learn when he or she is curious about a subject or when it directly involves them. Watch for the "teachable moments" in your child's day and maximize your telling then. When visiting Grandma in the hospital, prepare your child for what he might see

Even when I am the busiest, I stop and take time to care for my girls by giving them hugs. On days that I find it particularly hard to nurture them, I like to use situations to get through to them like gardening. I tell them how they need to care for the soil, seeds, seedlings, plants, and produce. Or we play with dolls and talk about caring for them in a tender, loving way.

— ❧ —

and remind him to use eye contact and ask questions so that Grandma will feel special. When preparing for a holiday, take a minute or two to explain the significance of the celebration, focusing especially on the meaning for your child.

Repeat important lessons

Children learn best through repetition. They memorize readily as youngsters. Especially words. Bible verses memorized as preschoolers are the ones that come back to them as adults. The same is true for a family's most important values. Many children learn little ditties because they are repeated often, like the Golden Rule: Do unto others as you would have them do unto you.

Tailor your telling to your child's age level

As a single parent, I realize my daughter consistently needs to feel loved and safe. Since I am her only example, she needs directions (which are rules of life for a child). She also needs to know I'm here, that I'll try to understand, and that she can trust me.

— ❧ —

Children are ready for certain pieces of information at specific ages. Take your child's moral, cognitive, and social development level into consideration before launching into a subject. For example, if she is only able to understand *good* means *what is pleasant* and *bad* means *what is painful* in her moral development, she probably won't understand that God loves criminals. At a young age, she will not understand the difference between being truthful and being tactful.

GETTING TO THE HEART
OF SHOW-ME-AND-TELL-ME LOVE

Many years ago, a popular book came out entitled *All I Really Needed to Know I Learned in Kindergarten* by Robert Fulghum. The kindergarten lessons included such helpful things as "Share everything; play fair; and say you're sorry when you hurt somebody." As important as these lessons are, that book communicates another great truth: children learn life's most basic and foundational lessons in their early years. These lessons are imprinted on their hearts and in their minds for life. As moms, we have a great privilege and responsibility to participate in this guiding process and meet their need for Show-Me-and-Tell-Me Love.

Love Handles

LOVE HANDLE #1:

Twelve Basic Lessons Worth Repeating

- Be honest.
- Set goals and work quietly and systematically toward them.
- Assign a task to yourself.
- Never give up.
- Be confident that you can make a difference.
- Don't ever stop learning and improving.
- Slow down and live.
- Choose your friends carefully.
- Be a can-do and will-try person.
- Try to live in the present.
- You are in charge of your own attitude.
- Always remember that you are never alone.[12]

LOVE HANDLE #2:

Your Child's Readiness for Guidance—
Age-Appropriate Development

Familiarize yourself with the various stages of mental, social, and moral development to be better equipped to guide your child appropriately.

Mental development

Jean Piaget theorized that children progress through the following periods along the path of mental development.

Birth to two years: Your child encounters his world in terms of action. There is lack of object permanence. When someone is out of sight, in the child's mind, he no longer exists. (No wonder he cries when Mom and Dad leave for a night out!) As the child learns to control his own body during the first two years of his life, he acquires the ability to mentally represent objects that are no longer present physically.

Two to seven years: The child encounters his world in terms of thoughts. With the emergence of language, the child continues to represent his world mentally. But his thinking is dominated by his own perspective. (When a six-year-old thinks she is right, there is no persuading her otherwise.)

Social development

Erik Erickson suggested that our psychological development progresses through eight stages, which are the result of an interaction between our biological needs and the social forces we encounter in everyday life. The first three stages happen between birth and about five years.

- Stage 1 (birth to one year): Trust vs. mistrust
  Can I trust the world? If Mom leaves, will she return? If I cry, will my needs be met?

- Stage 2 (two to three years): Autonomy vs. shame and doubt
  Can I control my own behavior? Can I learn to obey? Can I stop this tantrum, keep my bed dry, eat my vegetables?

- Stage 3 (four to five years): Initiative vs. guilt
  Can I explore my limits and become independent of my parents? Will mom answer me if I ask "why" again?

Moral development

Lawrence Kohlberg states evidence to suggest that morality (ideals or rules that govern human conduct) develops in steps. Here are the steps for preschoolers:

Level One—Pre-moral—birth to seven years

Step 1: Good equals what is pleasant. Bad equals what is painful. Rules are obeyed in order to avoid painful punishment.

Step 2: Right and wrong are judged on the basis of what pleases (and usually pleases the self). Rules are obeyed to obtain rewards and have favors returned.[13]

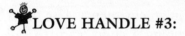

LOVE HANDLE #3:

Teaching Basic Survival Skills

Children should be able know when they need help and how to get it by acquiring these skills before the need arises. This teaching can be done in calm situations, so as not to frighten them, but to equip them. Here are some suggestions:

- Seek out "safe haven" homes in your neighborhood. Some homes display a National Crime Prevention Program decal which identifies it as a home that will help children who are frightened or lost. Others show a "Helping Hands" decal. Meet together as neighbors and agree to be safe haven homes for children who need help.
- While walking or driving around your neighborhood or town, point out safe places and safe havens. For instance, tell your child that if he is ever walking and feels scared or confused, he can go to the home of a neigh-

bor, to any house displaying the "Officer McGruff" or
"Helping Hands" decal, or to a convenience store, fire
station, library, or office building.

- Especially if being harassed by another child, have your
child find and ask an adult for help. This is an exception
to the rule about not talking to strangers.

- Play "what if" games with your child to teach skills.
"What if we got separated in the grocery store or the
shopping mall?" "What if I didn't show up when I said
I would pick you up at preschool?" "What if someone
knocks on the door, and I'm asleep or in the shower?"
This game can teach children some safe and appropriate choices of response when dealing with problems.

- Teach phone skills. Disconnect your phone and teach
children how to dial 911 in an emergency. Use other
people to role-play in helping a child learn to call
Daddy at work. List important phone numbers by the
phone. Even three-year-olds can learn to dial someone
for help in an emergency.

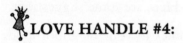

LOVE HANDLE #4:

Model and Teach Compassion

We teach children compassion by showing and telling
them how to help others. Here are some suggestions for projects that both model and teach about helping others:

- Help your child find opportunities to earn money to
buy canned goods to donate to a relief agency or directly to a needy family. (Call a local church or check the
yellow pages for agencies.) Have the child help pick out
coupons you can use to save money at the grocery store

and then give that money to the child to buy canned goods. Let the child help deliver the canned goods.

- Start a toy collection at home and in the neighborhood for children with no toys. Clean up the donated toys. Encourage the giving of good toys.

- Collect old videos in good condition and deliver them to a children's ward in a hospital, family services shelter, or a community center.

- Call a nursing home in your area and ask if you and your child can visit. Get the names of some people who don't get many visitors. Take your family dog if the rest home permits. Or take snacks your child can pass out.

- Put a map near your dining room table and mark the countries mentioned in the news or the ones where your church sends missionaries. Pray for people in those countries. Get the names and addresses of missionaries in those countries and let your child write a letter or draw a picture and dictate some words of encouragement that you write down.

- Volunteer to do yard work such as raking leaves or shoveling snow for an elderly neighbor.

- Clean up litter in an area in a local park.

**LOVE HANDLE #5:**

Turn a Walk into a Talk

The everyday activities we share with our children have lots of lessons tucked into them, whether it's a trip to a grocery store or the experience of making cookies together. Taking a walk gives an excellent opportunity for a talk about what you see. Author Pat Hershey Owen describes various kinds of walks:

We developed a variety of adventure-observation walks named by the children. Then, when we decided to go for a walk, we'd choose one that fit the day and our mood. Some days we'd take a "color walk." We would choose a color before leaving home, then see how many things we could find of that color. This helped to sharpen the children's color perception.

Another was the "vehicle walk." The children would ride tricycles or wagons, or take their pull and push toys. A word of caution. This walk is not for days when patience is fleeting. On one of our walks, we stopped to watch two birds building their nest. Later, I was telling a friend about the birds when Keith spoke. "Yep, we were work watching." Thus our "work watching" walks came into being. Perhaps the workers we observed would be ants scurrying to an ant hill, a squirrel gathering nuts, a spider weaving a web, or men working on streets or building. But whatever we watched, we always returned home with a greater admiration for God's creatures.[14]

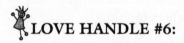

LOVE HANDLE #6:

Develop Critical Thinking Skills

In her book *Media Alert! 200 Activities to Create Media-Savvy Kids,* Sue Lockwood Summers suggests activities to help children develop and use critical thinking skills, especially as these skills apply to questioning, analyzing, and evaluating the messages they receive from mass media such as television, music, movies, radio, and newspapers. "Even a four-year-old can discuss his media world and analyze cartoons, cereal boxes, and picture book characters," she claims.[15]

Here are some suggested activities for preschoolers through kindergartners:

- Talk with child about TV commercials. Ask:
    Why are they on TV?
    What are the ads trying to do?
    Which ones does the child like/dislike?
    Why are some more appealing than others?
- Look at cereal boxes, book covers, or magazine ads:
    Which ones look most interesting?"
    What catches the child's attention?
- Compare a product (food item, clothing, or toy) with its TV ad:
    How does the item really look, taste, or function?
    Did the ad make it seem better than it really is?
- Talk back to the television!
    If content of TV program or commercial is false or offensive, say so out loud!
    If content of TV program or commercial is true or appropriate, say so out loud![16]
- Read a picture book to children, showing all of the illustrations. After reading the book, ask questions about the content, the sequence, the characters, the plot, and the illustrations. Discuss specific details of the illustrations. Review the story, especially the characters, sequence, consequences, and special moments.[17]

LOVE HANDLE #7:

Guide Your Child's TV Watching

- Know when your child is watching TV.
- Know what your child is watching.
- Allow your child to watch specific programs instead of watching to pass time.

- View and discuss some programs as a family.
- Don't watch television during meals.
- Connect television to reading. Relate a TV subject to a book and then read about it.

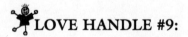

LOVE HANDLE #8:

Teaching Problem-Solving Techniques

- Ages 1–2: Children solve problems at this age by using all their senses and by imitating. They are curious, and by age two, they start asserting their independence. Help them learn problem-solving techniques by "thinking aloud" as you solve problems. Give them age-appropriate items to touch, smell, taste, and listen to. Tap into their quest for independence by giving them choices when solving problems.
- Ages 3–5: Children ages three to five try to solve problems by touching and doing. Three-year-olds may be less assertive than two-year-olds; they may try to get you to solve their problems for them. But four-year-olds are usually more aggressive and anxious to try their own problem-solving skills. Provide opportunities for them to solve problems, and again, give them choices whenever possible. Define boundaries and appropriate solutions. Praise their skills.

LOVE HANDLE #9:

Kindergarten Readiness

Here are some suggested skills most children should have before they enter kindergarten.

Academic:

- Know full name, address, and phone number
- Know age and birthday
- Be able to speak fluently and clearly
- Answer questions by using complete sentences
- Count objects from one to ten orally
- Recognize and name the eight basic colors
- Listen to a story and answer simple questions about it
- Follow simple directions
- Have some grasp of basic concepts such as up, down, beside, between, in, out, under, over, above, same, different, large, small, left, and right

Body/Motor Skills:

- Work a zipper
- Tie shoes
- Put on and take off boots
- Hang clothes up
- Ascend and descend stairs correctly
- Manipulate scissors, pencil, and crayon
- Cover nose and mouth when coughing or sneezing
- Use a drinking fountain correctly
- Go to bathroom alone

LOVE HANDLE #10:

Learning to Love Reading and Writing

Our culture is organized for people who read and write well. Success in school and business depends upon it. We can guide and encourage our children to enjoy reading and writing.

- Take a child to the library regularly. Let him pick out books. Attend story hour.
- The more stories you read out loud, the more your child enjoys reading and writing.
- Praise your child for his efforts to read or write.
- Keep the tools of writing around. Paper, jumbo pencils, crayons, and computers all encourage children to write.
- Show off their writing. Put the paper on the refrigerator or send it to Grandma. Give value to your child's effort.

MOM READING:

The ABC's of School Success, Elaine McEwan
A Cure for the Growly Bugs and Other Tried-and-True Tips for Moms,
    Mary Beth Lagerborg
Lord, Bless My Child, William and Nancie Carmichael
Making the Most of Your Child's Teachable Moments, Wanda B. Pelfrey
The Measure of Our Success, Marian Wright Edelman
Mom to Mom, Elisa Morgan
Raising Kids Who Turn Out Right, Tim Kimmel
Ready for Kindergarten, Sharon Wilkins
Schooling Options, Elaine McEwan
Unlocking Your Child's Learning Potential, Cheri Fuller
The Read-Aloud Handbook, Jim Trelease

LAP READING:

The Berenstain Bears Visit the Dentist, Stan and Jan Berenstain
The Berenstain Bears Learn About Strangers, Stan and Jan Berenstain
A Children's Book of Virtues, William J. Bennett
A Family Garden of Christian Virtues, Susan Lawrence
Uncle Willy's Tickles, Marcie Aboff

Six

Respect:
Let-Me-Be-Me Love

Come on, Gracie! We're supposed be at the Jacobson's house right now!" Glenna called out to her daughter. She thought she'd planned pretty well for this Saturday morning across-town journey to her girlfriend's. It was just a baby shower with a few of her old co-workers, but they hadn't seen Gracie for some time, and Glenna was anxious to show her off. So she'd laid out Gracie's red-and-white jumper, white tights, and red patent-leather shoes. She loved how Gracie looked in that outfit, especially with a matching red-and-white bow in her hair.

At almost four years old, though, Gracie was showing more and more signs of having a mind of her own, so Glenna had given her space to dress herself in her room alone. But now it was getting late. "Gracie, Sweetie, bring your toy bag and maybe that little white sweater too," she advised as she hurried down the hall toward her daughter's bedroom.

In the doorway, Glenna halted, catching her breath in surprise. There stood Gracie before her mirror, decked out in her white tights and red shoes, but not the red-and-white jumper. Instead she wore her ballerina outfit—a fluffy pink tutu with sparkly sequins—a smile of cherubic confidence spread across her cheeks. She clutched her toy bag and sweater in her chubby hands. "Okay, Mommy. I'm ready!" she announced.

Glenna surveyed her daughter, a head-to-toe cloud of pink poof anchored to the carpet with white-tighted legs stuffed into red patent-leather shoes. *No way!* she thought as she imagined the response of her friends when she and Gracie arrived at the shower. *What will they think of me if I let my daughter wear a pink tutu to an adult party?* She cringed slightly at the thought.

"Gracie, Sweetheart, what happened to that little jumper I laid out for you?" Glenna asked, trying to sound nonchalant.

"That dress doesn't make me feel pretty today, Mommy! I feel prettier in this! Don't you think I look pretty in this, Mommy?" Gracie hesitated, searching her mother's expression for approval.

Glenna felt the familiar tension of conflicting emotions. On the one hand, she wanted to tell Gracie she looked totally inappropriate and that people might laugh at her tutu. But then Glenna realized this was her problem, not Gracie's. She had built up an expectation about how Gracie should look in her red-and-white outfit when they arrived at the party; she anticipated that her friends would not only admire her child, but Glenna too, for being such a good mother.

On the other hand, she had to admit that Gracie did look pretty, not so much because of her outfit but because of the confidence that oozed from the satisfaction of making her own choice. It was as if Gracie were clarifying her own identity and defining her personal space through the selection of this outfit, stating to her mother and to any others, "This is me today! And I like me! I hope you do too!" She seemed totally free of both self-consciousness and self-centeredness.

All at once, Glenna made her own choice. Swallowing her expectations of a grand entrance and color-coordinated statement to her friends, she embraced her daughter's statement about who she was today.

"You do look pretty, Gracie!" she told her daughter with a smile. "Let's go."

R-E-S-P-E-C-T!

Children need respect, a Let-Me-Be-Me Love that meets their need to know they are valued for just exactly who they are. And who they can become. Children gain great confidence when they have the freedom and space to grow in their own unique way. They become more fully themselves when their method of learning is honored, their opinion heard, and their emotions understood.

But what a challenge to meet this need consistently and effectively—mostly because the child's need for respect often bumps into many of our own needs as moms. We need to know that we are doing okay as mothers. We want the approval of others. So we want our children to look the way we think they should look, or act the way we think they should act. We buck up and resist when they do not, because we fear that others might judge us as mothers based on our children's appearance or actions. In the face of these conflicts, we face a choice: Which need will we choose to meet—our child's need for respect or our own need for control, for a good performance, for affirmation as a mother?

Giving your child Let-Me-Be-Me Love requires an effort of the will, and often a retooling of thinking.

LET ME BE ME

Several components come together in meeting a child's need for this kind of love. A child verbalizes the need for respect as Let-Me-Be-Me Love, and if we want to meet this need, that's exactly what we have to learn to do: Let our children be who they are. That means knowing and understanding them, under-standing ourselves, and accepting both. Let's look at each part.

Know and Understand Your Child

How well do you know and understand your child? Re-spect begins by getting to know the unique child under your care. What is her favorite color? How does he respond to new situations? Is she a morning or night person?

I like to remind my kids of their unique-ness. I tell them that they have designer genes and that there's no one else like them. The truth is, God made them just the way they are.

— ta —

In his book *You and Your Child,* Chuck Swindoll states that get-ting to know your child is the single most helpful secret about child rear-ing that he can pass on to parents. But he also warns that it takes time and effort. A mother doesn't automati-cally know her child just because she has conceived, carried, and given birth to that child.

According to Swindoll, every child has "a bent, a set of char-acteristics already established. The bent is fixed and determined be-fore he is given over to our care. The child is not, in fact, a pliable piece of clay. He has been set; he has been bent. And the parent who wants to train this child correctly will discover that bent!"[1]

While a mother can underline and shape the "bent" of her child, she cannot completely change it. A child's bent is a child's personhood. Study the unique construction of your child as you would any other fascinating subject and then apply what you discover to the way you mother. Below are some characteristics to study.

Your child's personality

Each individual has a unique personality. Even within a family, some children are similar while others are polar opposites. Is your child introverted or extroverted? Does he make decisions based on thoughts or feelings? What are her talents and interests? Is she strong-willed or compliant? A peacemaker? An encourager? A helper?

A proverb in the Bible advises, "Train a child in the way he should go, and when he is old he will not turn from it." The key here is "the way he should go." Obviously there is a "right way," defined by biblical principles, such as the honest way, the way of wisdom, or the way defined by the Ten Commandments. But each child also has his own uniqueness imprinted into his soul and heart. Respecting your child means learning about this imprint and getting to know his personality—his way or his bent.

Your child's birth order

You can get to know your children better by understanding the role their birth order plays in who they are today and will be tomorrow. Birth order makes a difference in who we are and how we approach life.

Firstborn children are often perfectionists, critical, driven, successful under pressure, organized, on top of things, inflexible, scholarly, problem-solvers, list-makers, leaders, and self-starters. Many times the difficulty a mom has with her first child is in the areas where her own weaknesses lie. Perhaps you struggle with junk food addition. You may overreact when your child asks for candy, candy, candy! Or maybe you have a lazy streak and are uncomfortable when your child chooses television over outside activities.

Middle children are often "contradictions" of the firstborn. In an attempt to establish their own identities, they will probably be somewhat the opposite of the older child. Often middle children feel a bit "lost" in their families and are more apt to look to their friends for identification and self-worth. They make wonderful team players and often select professions where they can care for others.

Those born last are the "babies" of the family. Usually un-inhibited, affectionate, and outgoing, they have a burning desire to make a contribution to the world but are only too aware they are the youngest, smallest, and weakest. They often make wonderful salespeople and charming entertainers.

While birth order implications are complex and individual, their basic principles can provide insight into your child.

Your child's learning style

Children learn in their own way. Some are visual learners, deriving information from what they see. Others prefer auditory learning, taking in insights from listening. Still others learn by doing. You can identify your child's learning style by testing and observing. Teach him how to do a task on a computer. Does he learn best by being told how to do it, by watching you do it, or by doing it himself?

Understanding our child's learning style and then adjusting guidance accordingly can be a daunting task for a mother. Educational expert and mom Cynthia Tobias comments that "one learning style can be almost as different from another as two foreign languages are from each other."[2]

It's tough to step out of your own visual learning style and guide your child through the listening learning style. But what a valuable method for communicating respect, plus helping your child succeed in life! The basis of much of communication and love is learning to speak the language of another, reaching across our differences, from our world into theirs, to say that we care in a way that is meaningful not necessarily to us, but to them.

Your child's feelings

Just like moms, children have feelings. And they need help in understanding and processing them. This isn't always comfortable or easy. Feelings can be inconvenient, confusing, and embarrassing, especially our children's feelings and especially when they are expressed in public.

Learning to read and respect your child's feelings is vital for the child's emotional health. Randolph Sanders writes,

I try to understand my daughter's motives and what she's thinking and feeling. For example, I always squat down to be at her eye level when she has something to explain.

— ❧ —

I hate when parents say to their children, "Oh, you're not scared" or "Oh, you're not hurt" or "You don't feel that way." We shouldn't trivialize their feelings.

— ❧ —

Our feelings, and those of our children, are real, and we deny them at our own risk. When we can learn to identify our feelings, and help our children identify theirs, we give those feelings a name. Then the feelings have less power over us. When we deny feelings like anger or hurt, they become mysterious seething caldrons that lurk below the level of conscious awareness yet still wreak havoc. Once we've named our feelings, our head finally gets some control over our heart.[3]

Do you see the pattern? Learn to identify your feelings. Help your children identify theirs. Then come to understand what is behind the feelings. In following such a process, we honor our children and their right to feel. Such emotional training will assist our children in all the interpersonal interactions they encounter, whether with siblings or future spouses. Knowing your children means knowing their feelings are legitimate, even when you don't agree, they don't make sense, or they are negative or inconvenient.

Family expert John Drescher believes that there is a "vital relationship between listening to children's concerns when they are young and the extent to which these children—when they are in their teens—will share their concerns with their parents."[4]

Respect for your child's feelings begins early and pays big dividends later in your interactions with your older child.

Your child's age-appropriate development

Respect for the challenges your child faces by age is crucial in Let-Me-Be-Me Love. It helps to know the appropriate cognitive developmental tasks.

A two-year-old should be gaining some success in the issue of separation from you, as mother. Yet, he will waffle back and forth. Sometimes he will hang by your leg, then walk off by himself, and then return to find you again. If you've moved to another room, he will likely get angry because he wants to control where you are in his life so that he can risk stepping out and away from you.

Similarly, a five-year-old gathers information through questions, questions, questions. Your patient answering will help your child build confidence in her mental abilities and the ability to test and try in her world.

Children who are adopted may struggle to understand their identity at various developmental stages, yet in other stages these same children may evidence very little confusion or pain. Your preparedness for the necessary processing can assist and provide the space and understanding needed by the adopted child.

I yelled at my six-year-old one day because he forgot to take off his shoes and tracked dirt across my new carpet. He had been excited to show me something. He said, "Mom, I'm still a kid and haven't learned to remember everything yet."

— ❧ —

Respecting your children means knowing which developmental stage they are in and adjusting your expectations and input appropriately.

Your child's special needs

Many children have needs that fall outside of what textbooks call "normal." Downs Syndrome. Physical disabilities. Learning disorders. Do you know if your child struggles with such a need? And if so, do you understand how to help?

For example, children with learning disabilities are often able to handle only one task at a time. Perhaps we can eat a bagel, read a newspaper, and carry on a conversation all at the same time. But for a child with a learning disability, each of these tasks could be a cognitive task, requiring independent thinking. To expect a child with a disorder to complete three cognitive tasks at once is completely unrealistic. Each piece must be broken down and handled separately.

One mother wrote of her struggle to understand and deal with her five-year-old with Attention Deficit Disorder. "I tried rewards, coaxing, begging, forcing. I searched for help with medication and behavior modification training. Then I realized that all my efforts were being perceived as rejection by my daughter, conveying the message that she wasn't good enough. That new understanding helped us turn an important corner."

Sometimes the needs of our child are special because they involve great mental or physical challenge for us and for them. Alfred Lord Tennyson penned this poem, tenderly touching the challenge of loving and understanding a retarded or disabled child:

> I hold you here, root and all, in my hand
> but if I could understand
> what you are, root and all,
> I should know what God and man is.[5]

Respect comes when we get to know any special need of our child and adjust ourselves to meet that need.

It's been said that "knowing is the most profound kind of love."[6] We give a rich flavor to Let-Me-Be-Me Love when we get to know, really know, and understand our child.

Know and Understand Yourself

When you get to know your child, you begin to discover ways in which this child is both similar and different from you; how this child both resembles and is opposite to you. Such discoveries often evoke puzzling responses from within us as mothers. We sometimes discover where parts of them bump into parts of us. Or where a child's need for Let-Me-Be-Me Love bumps into a mother's need for a child to be "who I want you to be right now." As we hit those bumps, we sometimes discover things about ourselves we don't really like. It helps to stop and look at some examples of those bumpy places.

Freedom to explore who my children are is difficult for me because it often interferes with my agenda. For example, my son loves to explore how things work. But this kind of play can be very messy, and there are many times when I don't want to indulge him because I don't want to deal with the mess.

— ❧ —

"I may expect too much of my child."

She's three. She gets up at six every morning. We're tired from the new baby who wakes every four hours. She pads into the room, to the side of our bed and shakes our shoulder, asking for breakfast. We tell her to get some cereal and juice and let Mommy sleep. When we make it downstairs a half hour later, she's sitting in front of the TV, her fist in the box of Frosted Flakes, with crumbs spread out like confetti all around her on the carpet. A dribbly trail of sticky yellow juice leads from the kitchen counter across the floor to the table where a juice cup sits with yellow rings growing around it. In our fatigue and frustration, we lose it. She cries and says, "But Mommy, you told me to!" Oops. Ouch. She obeyed, in an age-appropriate way, but we had an unrealistic ex-

I signed my son up for indoor soccer and every game he just stood on the court looking around. After several weeks of my being frustrated, he reminded me he never wanted to play in the first place but that I had pushed him into it.

— ❧ —

pectation that just because she's the older child now, she should be able to get her own breakfast without making a mess. A bunch of mixed up, misunderstood feelings. Hers and yours.

"I have to admit that I'm disappointed with my child."

He's slow. He should be walking by now. All the other children his age started walking months ago. The doctor says he is behind in his development. Maybe something more is wrong. Who knows? What will this mean for the future? We're an athletic and fast-moving family of go-getters. How will we learn to slow down for this child?

Or perhaps she seems behind mentally. She doesn't "get" her colors! She can't keep her numbers straight. She may have a learning disability. How will she get by? Will we be able to share our love of books with her?

"Don't tell anyone, but I don't really like my child."

She's giggly and loud. We're reserved and quiet. She embarrasses us with her loud, tomboy sounds. We feel the need to make up excuses. She isn't soft-spoken and feminine like the little girl we wanted her to be. She doesn't like music. Or reading. Or sit-still activities. Instead she likes to be the center of attention. She likes people, loud ones and lots of them.

The truth is, moms sometimes have a hard time accepting their kids the way they are. That's why grandparenting is such a

*As my daughters get older, I am strug-
gling with accepting them for who they
are. Before, they were always little "clones"
of me. But they don't have the same tastes
or areas of success as I did at school. I
sometimes struggle with the question,
"Why is she only average in math? I was
an 'A' student."*

— ❧ —

joy. Grandparents auto-
matically accept their
grandchildren.   They
smile with patient, un-
derstanding love when a
child spills milk or dis-
covers an interest in bi-
ology or wants to wear a
pink tutu to a baby
shower. They have noth-
ing at stake in their grandchild's choices. They have already trav-
eled the turf of defining themselves by their children's actions.
In wisdom, most have learned to surrender their own desires in
order to encourage the uniqueness in their children.

Let-Me-Be-Me Love requires a choice from a mother: Am
I pushing for what I want my child to be, or will I get to know
and support who my child is? Occasionally those two overlap.
But all too often, those two choices bump into each other. Respect comes when we make the choice to sacrifice our own desires or template for the blueprint God has imprinted in the
hearts and souls of our children.

Accept Your Child—and Yourself

Your child is not you. Your child is a little person in his
own right, with his own personality, learning style, birth order,
feelings, developmental needs, and special needs.

In his book *Unconditional Love*, John Powell explains the
kind of respect our children need from us as their moms.

> You can be whoever you are, express all your thoughts and
> feelings with absolute confidence. You do not have to be
> fearful that love will be taken away. You will not be pun-
> ished for your openness or honesty. There is no admission

price to my love, no rental fees or installment payments to be made. There may be days when disagreements and disturbing emotions may come between us. There may be times when psychological or physical miles may lie between us. But I have given you the word of my commitment. I have set my life on a course. I will not go back on my word to you. So feel free to be yourself, to tell me of your negative and positive reactions, of your warm and cold feelings. I cannot always predict my reactions or guarantee my strength, but one thing I do know and I do want you to know: I will not reject you! I am committed to your growth and happiness. I will always love you.[7]

Note that respecting our children doesn't mean that every response we offer will be perfect, nor even adequate at times. We will run into our bumps, but when we recognize and accept that fact, we move through or around those bumps more easily.

Respecting our children means holding before us the choice to let them be themselves rather than who we've determined they should be. It means honoring their unique individuality and separateness.

My kids need to know that I will take the time to explain what I need and that I will listen to what they need. My son has said to me, "Mommy, you don't understand. You are not listening to me." I ask him to help me understand. I want him to learn that being patient takes time, and I will take the time to learn that.

— ❧ —

RESPECTFUL TREATMENT

Family expert Ron Hutchcraft concludes that "our primary feelings of whether we are okay or not okay come from our mother and father. As adults, we are still carrying around the self-worth or self-worthless tapes our parents recorded in our hearts. Today, we are making tapes for our son or daughter to play back wherever they go."[8] So how do we demonstrate respect to our one-year-old, our two-and-a-half-year-old, our almost five-year-old? Seems like a big task, doesn't it?

I try to listen to my child's clock when I schedule my day.

— ❧ —

Perhaps the easiest way to demonstrate respect is to offer what you yourself would interpret as respect to your child. When a child feels respected he, in turn, learns to respect others around him. In many simple, daily ways we can demonstrate respect to our little ones.

Give Them Space

For their personhood to grow and develop, children need space of their own. Physically, this means their own toy box, their own desk, their own plate or cup, their own stuffed animal, their own bed and toothbrush. Of course, many families aren't able to provide extensively for physical space for each and every child. But all families can give at least some items that define space and separate out one individual from another. Involve your child in the creation and upkeep of his own spaces. Let her organize them, rearrange them, and decorate and label them as she likes.

We knock on doors before entering bedrooms, and we try to honor opinions for food, activities, and clothing. We also try to remember to keep the main thing the main thing.

— ❧ —

A space of their own includes emotional space as well. Children shouldn't be forced to share their feelings or thoughts. Communication is a choice given in response to trust. Respecting their privacy reinforces the value of an individual's choices.

Be Polite

Say "Please," "Thank you," "Excuse me," and "I'm sorry" regularly and you will go a long way to build into your child's need for respect. Don't embarrass them. Don't call them disrespectful names or tell them to shut up. Treat them as politely as you treat your friends. Good manners communicate respect.

Occasionally, I'll shout at my son when I'm upset about something. He'll say, with a hurt look in his eyes, "Don't shout at me! Just tell me!"

— ❧ —

When you've made a mistake, instead of bemoaning the error, view it as an opportunity to underline the value of your child. When children watch their moms learn from mistakes, they are freed to learn from their own as well.

Gary Smalley suggests five steps to apologizing that communicate respect.

1. Become tenderhearted. This communicates value and compassion to our child.
2. Increase understanding. When we determine to understand our child's pain and how she has interpreted our offense, we reach out with love.
3. Recognize the offense. Admit where you were wrong, clearly and honestly.
4. Attempt to touch. Appropriate and gentle touch can help you gauge whether or not the child is beginning to forgive you, while, at the same time, meets the child's need to know that you love him.
5. Seek forgiveness. Asking for forgiveness is directly respectful and honors the one you have wronged.[9]

Converse with Them

A conversation involves both talking and listening. We can communicate respect with our children when we both listen and talk.

When my daughter was about three, she kept tugging on my pant leg while I was trying to do the dishes. I kept trying to push her away so I could get the kitchen clean. After several attempts she finally yelled, "Please look me in the eyes when I'm talking, Mommy!" What our children have to say is just as important as what we have to say!

— ❧ —

When your child has something to say to you, open up your very being to take in her meaning. Author Ken Gire writes, "The way we show respect is to give it a second look, a look not of the eyes but of the heart. But so often we don't give something a second look because we don't think there is anything there to see."[10] Real listening requires that we zip our lips shut on what we want to say and honor the expression of our children.

My children sometimes say, "You just don't understand," to which I reply, "Not yet, but can you help me?"

— ❧ —

But that's not all. Conversation also involves talking. How greatly we can encourage our children by telling them often and clearly how greatly we value them! Pastor Charles Stanley reminds us that "it is not what you *think* that will have an impact on your children; it is what you *communicate*."[11]

Honor Their Efforts

If my daughter insists on trying something, I usually let her, even if it sounds yucky. The other day she mixed chocolate syrup and whipped cream for a special beverage that she decided wasn't all that great.

— ❧ —

Sometimes our children make pictures with crayons or they hand over a clump of clay and call it a "kitty cat." It is their treasure, and they want it to be ours. They often make messes as they create their masterpieces. Often a mother's need to keep the house clean bumps into a child's need to be creative or explore these interests. The following poem called, "Cleaning Up," describes this mother-vs.-child need.

> Crayoned papers cut in squares
> Grains of rice in a cup
> Magazine coupons
>   and many small rocks.
> Bottle caps, plastic and metal,
> Five pennies and a ziplock
>   full of autumn leaves
> A popsicle stick
> Clutter
> fills my coffee table,
>   My small living room
> tucked in odd places, hidden there
> Like shredding cash, I throw away
>   your treasures
> Till, tearful, you remind me
> that beauty is in the eye of the
>   Beholder
> and I have plundered your castle,
>   your home.[12]

Enjoy Them

In her book *Getting Out of Your Kids Faces and Into Their Hearts,* Valerie Bell offers up a phrase we might all incorporate into our mothering: loyal delight. She writes, "Acceptance must be mixed with a large dose of something that, for lack of an appropriate word, I'll call *loyal delight* in who that child is. A parent's job is to celebrate the child, *as he or she is.*"

She goes on to define certain characteristics as inclusive in this quality:

- A high degree of satisfaction. That means you forego the need to have your child be the most popular, the most talented, the most gifted. You express high contentment and gratification with exactly who your child is. Are you glad you had this child? Would you have traded her for any other? Why not tell her so?
- To take great pleasure. Another way of saying this is to think of conveying the idea that your child has the power to make your day, your week, your life—that you enjoy being his or her parent.
- To give keen enjoyment. Let your eyes light up when your children are around. Laugh more. Tell them how empty and quiet it is when they're not there. Enjoy the things they bring to your life. Attend their activities, not as if they were compulsories for parents, but throw yourself into their lives. . . . Enjoy, enjoy, enjoy![13]

My children need to be treated with the same kind of respect and kindness that I use in treating my friends.

— ❧ —

Empower Them

I let my kids have their own opinions—I'm not always right. They are allowed to present their side of an issue as long as it is done with respect. They need to know I will listen and consider what they have to say.

— ❧ —

You show respect for your children by carefully balancing acceptance of who they are with encouragement to grow into all they can be. Balance is the key.

Encourage your children's strengths

Look carefully for attributes your child uniquely possesses and underline them as often as you see them manifested. "You're such a good listener!" "What a generous spirit you have!" "You are a leader of your whole class!" When you underline your child's strengths, you motivate him to embrace them and grow them.

> *There are attributes of each of our children's personalities that can be positive or negative, depending on how they use them. We try to show them the positive ways.*
>
> — ❧ —

Expect them to be all they can be

Family counselor John Rosemond advises that "respecting children involves accepting them for what they are, patiently nurturing them toward what they are becoming, and expecting a lot of them."[14] Let-Me-Be-Me Love is accepting who your child is while also underlining what he can be.

> *Get to know each of your children, so you can expect the best of them individually.*
>
> — ❧ —

GETTING TO THE HEART OF LET-ME-BE-ME LOVE

Our children come into this world imprinted with a special personality blueprint. As they grow, they start making statements about that personality. "I need Let-Me-Be-Me Love," they tell us with various expressions, through the way they act and dress and the choices they make. As moms, we have an opportunity to nurture and encourage this uniqueness as we seek to know and understand our children and accept them. As we meet their need for respect—for Let-Me-Be-Me Love—we encourage our children to reach their potential and become fully themselves.

Love Handles

LOVE HANDLE #1:

How Well Do You Know Your Child?

What is her favorite toy? Favorite book? Favorite TV program?

What is her best time of day?

Is he strong-willed or compliant?

Who is his best friend?

What embarrasses her?

What is her favorite song? Favorite color? Favorite food this week?

What is his greatest fear?

What makes her angry?

What would he like to be when he grows up?

What is her greatest strength?

What does he like to do when he is alone?

How does she learn best?

LOVE HANDLE #2:

Showing Respect for Your Child

Here are some ways to show respect for a child:

- Accept your child. Respect his developmental ability. Don't compare him to someone else.

- Allow and accept your child's feelings, even anger. Remember, your child has a right to feel his feelings.
- Share your feelings with your child.
- Don't expect more of your child than you do of yourself.
- Show patience with problems.
- Discipline in private.
- Don't complain about your child or the burdens of parenting in front of your child.
- Show an interest in his friends. Invite his friends to your house.
- Respect your child's secrets and needs for privacy.

LOVE HANDLE #3:

Identify Your Child's Learning Style

According to experts, we take in information in two ways: *concrete,* using our five senses; and *abstract,* using our intuition and imagination. We also order information and organize our lives in two ways: *sequential,* in a linear, step-by-step manner; and *random,* in chunks, with no particular sequence. These two ways of perceiving and ordering give us four learning style combinations. Everyone uses all four, but most of us are dominant in at least one or two.

Identifying and understanding your child's learning style not only helps them academically, but it can also help you avoid family conflicts. For instance, let's look at how different learners respond differently to a common problem: bedtime battles.

- A child who is a dominant Concrete Sequential may respond best to an established bedtime routine, including at least a two-minute warning to prepare before bedtime.
- You can help a dominant Abstract Sequential prepare for bed by starting early enough for the child to complete any necessary tasks to his or her satisfaction. Help set out the child's clothes and materials for the next day.

- Avoid bedtime battles with a dominant Abstract Random by setting a personal, close nighttime routine such as reading a book, having a quiet conversation, saying prayers, etc. Ask the child what will comfort him or her the most: a stuffed animal, a night-light, leaving the door open?
- Dominant Concrete Randoms should be allowed some negotiation on minor points like which bed, what pajamas, or which night-light. Be sure this child has lots of opportunities to burn up energy well before bedtime.[15]

LOVE HANDLE #4:

Allowing Your Child to Say No

When parents teach children that setting boundaries or saying no is bad, they are teaching them that others can do with them as they wish. Parents who do so are sending their children defenseless into a world that contains much evil. Evil in the form of controlling, manipulative, and exploitive people. Evil in the form of temptations.

To feel safe in such an evil world, children need to have the power to say things like:

- "No."
- "I disagree."
- "I choose not to."
- "Stop that."
- "It hurts."
- "It's wrong."
- "That's bad."
- "I don't like it when you touch me there."

Blocking a child's ability to say no handicaps that child for life.[16]

 **LOVE HANDLE #5:**

Picture a Special Future for Your Child

Long ago, parents bestowed a blessing upon a child by helping that child picture a special future. That process begins as we help our children recognize, accept, and celebrate their own uniqueness and strengths. Help them dream dreams. Expand their horizons. Set their sights. Here are some suggestions to help you shape a vision or give your child a window into his future.

- Notice and encourage your child's good qualities and strengths: a display of kindness to another, an ability to play soccer, an interest in books or music, a tenderness for animals. Help him feel good about being good at something.
- Play a pretend game with your child. Look into her eyes or ears or heart and pretend you can see things inside that represent special interests, even worries or fears. For instance, "I see a huge pile of something over there in the corner. It looks sweet, like a pile of sugar. Oh yes, it must be your sweetness and kindness to others."
- Give compliments on jobs well done. Pass on compliments from others.
- Write your child's name on a piece of paper posted on the refrigerator door. Every day for a week, write down positive comments or one-word descriptions of your child.
- Make up an encouraging acrostic, using each letter of your child's name.
- Once an interest is discovered in your child, raise her vision. If she likes music, take her to a concert. Encourage her to play an instrument. Listen to music together. Take time to explore her interest, even if it does not match your interest.

- Make a "Special Future" scrapbook or special photo album of pictures showing your child's unique interests or strengths.
- Write a poem or prayer that honors and affirms your child's strengths.

MOM READING:

The Birth Order Book, Kevin Leman
Born to Fly, Thom Black
Creative, Confident Children, Maxine Hancock
Different Children, Different Needs, Charles F. Boyd
Every Child Can Succeed, Cynthia Tobias
I'll Love You Forever, Norm and Joyce Wright
Kids Have Feelings Too! Norm Wright and Gary Oliver
Raising Adopted Children, Lois Ruskai Melina
The Way They Learn, Cynthia Tobias
The Whole Life Adoption Book, Jayne E. Schooler

LAP READING:

Alexander and the Horrible, Terrible, No Good, Very Bad Day, Judith Viorst
Horton Hears a Who, Dr. Seuss
I Am Me! Alexa Brandenberg
I Remember When I Was Afraid, Larry Libby
Mean Soup, Betsy Everitt
Tacky the Penguin, Helen Lester
The Treasure Tree, Gary and Norma Smalley and John and Cynthia Trent
Why Was I Adopted? Carole Livingston

seven

Play:
Play-With-Me Love

Whew!" Annie said out loud as she collapsed in a chair. The third load of wash was folded and put away—finally. It had been a loooonnng morning. Rainy. The boring kind of indoor day when her children, Kevin, six, and Laura, four, pestered her for ideas and involvement.

But she still had so much to do. Her parents were coming for the weekend, and she had to get groceries and pay the bills stacked up on her desk. And there on the coffee table sat a half-finished photo album surrounded by piles of pictures.

"Mommy! Can we make a blanket fort?!" Kevin appeared with his little sister as if from nowhere, eyes twinkling with excitement over the prospect. Predicting his mother's tired refusal before it was spoken, he zoomed ahead, describing all the benefits of blanket-fort-building, like he was a miniature marketing expert for blanket forts. "Oh please, please! Laura and I can do it all by ourselves. You don't have to do a thing. We'll get the blankets out of the closet, and we'll put them all back when we're done. And we'll be sooo quiet, Mommy, you can get lots of work done. Please? Can we? Please?" Laura punctuated her big brother's pleading words with little hops of enthusiasm at her mother's side.

Annie rolled her eyes and hesitated. "Oh, Kevin . . . I'm so tired, and I have so much more to do today."

"I know, Mommy, but Laura and I will do it all for you! Come on, Mommy, please?"

Annie's resolve evaporated. "Okay, but you have to clean it *all* up—okay?"

With that, the children whirled and sped to the closet where they tugged at blankets until they fell from the shelves in heaps about them. Giggling, they dragged them to the family room, dropped them in a pile, and ran for the kitchen chairs, which they positioned as pillars at four corners. Next they were laying flat blankets over chairs, pulling one end tight across a distance to lay atop another chair, whereupon the first part collapsed.

Worried, Kevin looked to his mother, who was already buried under a stack of bills and letters. Obviously they needed some safety pins. And if they needed safety pins, they needed her. Rolling her eyes a second time, Annie pushed her pile of paperwork aside, gathered up her tired body and announced with a huff, "I'll get the pins, Kevin." Returning, Annie stuck a handful in her mouth and began pulling and pinning the slippery blankets into place.

"Oh thank you, Mommy! Laura, come on, let's go in." And two little bodies disappeared inside the blanket fort. Annie could hear her children happily chatting away, nested into the blankets in their cozy hideaway.

"Oh, Mommy, come inside and see!" They both begged. Something inside Annie began to soften, and she got down on her hands and knees and crawled through a blanket-tunnel to a cozy little spot beside the coffee table. There she snuggled down beside her children, and suddenly the memories of her own childhood blanket forts began to overshadow the tug of her to-do list. In her mind, she heard the voices of her own little brother and sister. *Let's pretend that we're a grown-up family. I'm the mommy. And you be the baby. . . .* She remembered her own need to play as a child, and, with a pang, she recognized how she sometimes squelched this need in her children. Not today. Today she would embrace it.

"Okay, my children," she told them, nose-to-nose in the darkness. "Let's pretend that this fort is really a ship, and the rooms are the cabins!" Kevin and Laura opened their eyes wide with joy at their mother's spontaneous playfulness. "And we're here in the ship's library," she said, "so we need some books . . ." With that, Annie lifted the blanket, slithered out, and gathered an armload of library books and a flashlight. She returned and scrunched back into a spot between the two children, who laughed because her hair was sticking to the blanket-roof in static electric spikes. "Okay, let's read for a while, and then we'll have a picnic lunch in here," she announced. "Maybe, just maybe, we'll live in here *forever!*"

PLAY PLAYS A PART IN A CHILD'S DEVELOPMENT

At first glance, Play-With-Me Love might seem a bit frivolous to a busy, tired mother who struggles at times just to get through the day.

> *Little by little, my six-year-old and I are building a castle for his GI Joes out of boxes, egg cartons, and toilet paper rolls!*
>
> — ❧ —

Sure, we can make room for the obvious needs like Hold-Me-Close Love and Crazy-About-Me Love. But Play-With-Me Love seems to be a need that busy moms could let children meet on their own, without help from an adult. After all, children seem to play so naturally. Why focus specifically on meeting this need?

Because we as mothers must recognize the importance of play in a child's life, and our role in facilitating play times.

Play Is Child's Work

I bought laundry baskets (which we called delivery trucks and filled with pretend gas) for each of my children so they could each "deliver" laundry to different parts of the house. When they were young, we made a game out of finding pairs of socks in the unfolded laundry.

— ❧ —

From the time they awake in the morning until they lay their tired heads on their pillows at night, a child works through play. It is how they learn about life, and it plays an important part in the child's growth and development, as author and mother Miriam Huffman Rockness describes in her book *A Time To Play*. A child's play is "his means of discovering the world as well as himself. He formulates an understanding of the universe in which he lives, bit by bit, as he rambles and roams, looking, listening, tasting, touching, smelling. He discovers aspects of his temperament and personality by interacting with other children. . . . In the nonthreatening world of play, children can seek and try the unfamiliar; they can practice and master newly acquired skills."[1]

Play Creates Creativity and Stimulates Imagination

Two words in the English language uniquely spark creativity and imagination: "Let's pretend . . ."

With these two words, our children are launched into the exploration of their world. During the early years of life, we can actually stimulate their intelligence and capacity for later learning as we encourage them to use imagination and creative play. Albert Einstein, known for his intelligence, compared knowledge and imagination: "Imagination is more important than knowledge, for knowledge is limited, whereas imagination embraces the entire world."[2]

Children are naturally creative, but they often lose their creative flair as they grow up. "At the age of five, perhaps 90 percent of our children have high levels of creativity," says Marlene LeFever, who has written widely on the topic of creativity and children. "But that percentage drops to about 10 percent for elementary children. Only about 2 percent of the adult population has a high creativity level."[3]

Looking back over his years of parenting, William Coleman wishes

I get down on the floor with my youngest and his toys, and play cars or space ship or army men. We have great fun during these times.

— ❧ —

he had encouraged more creativity and played more "make believe" with his children in order to help them learn about faith. "The land of make-believe is excellent territory to learn about faith," he says. "It's just a short hop, skip, and a jump from fairy godmothers and elves to guardian angels. We were afraid we couldn't teach the difference between the pretend and the real. Today I know we could have. You have to believe before you can have faith."[4]

Play Allows Children to Be Children

Play allows a child to be a child and to embrace the things of childhood. In his book *The Hurried Child*, well-known author David Elkind warns us not to rush our children through childhood, with all its important developmental steps. He advises us not to push children to learn too soon or to become "miniature adults" while still children. Sometimes we do this subtly by encouraging our children to act "all grown up." Or by giving greater value to learning life skills than for playing. Elkind uses the

*Ever since my sons were babies, we've
chased each other around the house. Their
laughter filled the house and they always
begged for more.*

— ❧ —

example of programs at children's summer camps that have cut their "fun" offerings to give children more programs in foreign language, competitive sports, and computer training. "The change in programs of summer camps reflects the new attitude that the years of childhood are not to be frittered away by engaging in activities merely for fun."[5]

Play Lets Children Grow Up to Be Healthier Adults

Adults need to integrate childlikeness into their lives. Knowing how and when to play and have fun is a skill all adults need in order to be healthy and well-balanced. A mom who believes she must finish all her work before she can go for a bike ride or play a game of cards or go swimming is a mom who will begin to feel stress in her life. If we nurture the childlikeness in our children *when they are children,* we help them develop a habit they need to grow up to be healthy adults.

Children themselves need recreation. The word *recreate* means "to restore, refresh, or create anew" and can mean "to restore in body or mind, especially after work, by play, amusement, or relaxation." During childhood we learn how to *re-create* through play. We learn the habit of playing, the balance of play and work, and the benefits play adds to our sense of well-being.

BUMPING INTO A "NO PLAY" ZONE

*like to sing and dance with my kids in
he kitchen while we're making meals.*

— ❧ —

Children need our encouragement and participation in their play times. Pediatrician Grace

Ketterman says, "Despite their preoccupation with their imaginary play, their efforts to help you work, and their many questions, preschoolers need you to play with them. Wrestling, tickling, blowing in their necks, and tousling their hair are all examples of physical touching that is so vital to the ongoing bonding process. Observe your child, though. When rough play is no longer fun for either you or your child, it's best to stop."[6]

But not all moms enjoy playing with their children. Some don't have time to play as much as their children want them to play. Others don't know how to play. Still others have needs that conflict with their child's needs for play. For these reasons, many moms bump into a "No Play Zone," coming up with excuses when it comes to meeting their children's needs through play.

"But I've Got Too Much to Do!"

The demands of our to-do lists often keep us from playing with our children. Errands. Deadlines. Bills. Phone calls. Obligations and shoulds and ought-tos. Age-old ditties drift through our minds, shaping our priorities and putting play at the bottom of our priorities. "Work first and play later." "Cleanliness is next to godliness." "Don't put off to tomorrow what you can do today." Play? No way. Not now. Not today.

The truth is, moms will always have something more to do. Even the best-intentioned mother who tells herself that she'll play as soon as she finishes this project or that task will always have trouble following through. If she saves play for when she finishes her work, she may never do it.

One mom reminded herself of the value of playing *now* through her poem, "Thank You, God, for Children":

> Thank you, God, for children.
> And toothpaste in the sink.
> For holes in knees

Of brand new jeans
And one more nighttime drink.

Thank you, God, for tiny feet
Who track dirt through the house.
For chocolate chips
And smiling lips,
and friends like Mickey Mouse.

For sticky hands and dirty socks
And toys strewn on the floor,
A lemonade stand,
The Ice Cream Man,
And treasures to explore.

Thank you, God, for little hands
With dandelion bouquets.
For good cartoons,
Birthday balloons,
For time we have to play.

Someday my house will quiet down
For now I will enjoy
The time each day
To run and play
With precious little boys.[7]

"But It'll Make a Mess!"

Many moms feel that children's play makes more work for us. If they get out the blankets or the Play-Doh or the stuff to make cookies, it'll make a mess. And we'll have to clean it up.

In her book *Wonderful Ways to Love a Child*, Judy Ford advises that "you can keep the messes in perspective when you remember that one of these days the kids will be gone, and you'll have the house all to yourself, and may sigh at the thought of those wet towels on the bathroom floor."[8]

As moms, messes sometimes feel like symbols of a loss of control, of unpredictability and of unfinished business in our lives. But we try to look past the "stuff" of a mess to what play can accomplish in the life of a child and try to see messes as symbols of creativity.

"But I'm Too Tired!"

No doubt, the mother of very young children faces exhaustion more frequently now than at any other time of her life. Up and down through the night. Pestered throughout the day. Juggling multiple tasks and roles as she seeks stability in the home. Besides the demands put on moms, we often struggle with the feelings of depression or confusion due to hormonal adjustments, changing identities, loneliness, or lack of regular physical exercise.

Being a mother of preschoolers is a wipe-out job. Most of us are too pooped to read a book, much less play. But rather than taking more from you, playing with your children can restore you. It's good for your kids and it's good for you. One mother proved this after an exhausting day in which she had taken her two feverish preschool-aged boys to the doctor and then to the drugstore for medicine. "My husband was working late, and the boys were irritable because they didn't feel good. I was irritable too because I'd been up most of the night with them. They started throwing stuffed animals across the living room, which annoyed me. I began to tell them to stop and sit in a time-out but then I remembered the advice to play with them more often. So I got down on their level and threw stuffed bunnies with them. After a few minutes, my youngest son turned to me and said, 'Mommy, I like you.' We all felt better after that."

"But I Don't Know How to Play!"

Growing up has a way of making us forget how to play or create fun in life. The responsibility of raising children can snuff out our own childlikeness. We get set in our ways and lose the ability to see and feel the wonder that children experience so naturally.

"Our lives are surrounded with such wonders," one writer writes, "but all too often we are blind to them. We fall into the habit of classifying objects, missing the uniqueness of each individual thing: a tree in the fog, for example. A dullness so easily descends upon our vision that we lose our sensitivity to life's simple wonders. We have grown into 'adults', we have seen too much and have become numb to the delicacy which surrounds us."[9]

I seem to take life and child-raising a little too seriously.

— ❧ —

Children can help moms remember that moms need play too. Watching our children at play re-creates our own childlikeness, awakening our qualities of youth, imagination, and creativity. Sometimes we need to stop and listen to the childlike nudges within us, and share our childlikeness with our own children by playing together. Patricia Sprinkle writes of the inspiration which comes from children:

To My Child:

How delighted you are with yourself! Having mastered a chair, you now want to scale the table. Every day you have to explore each piece of furniture to see what new abilities you have acquired since yesterday. And you are having such fun. When did I lose that self-delight? What happened to my awareness that every day I can do some things I have never been able to do before? What made me content to stop trying out yesterday's impossibilities to see if they could be done today? Does being grown up mean being content with "what is" when we could be striving for "what could be?" Inspire me, Child, to stretch my world as you stretch yours.[10]

ENTERING THE PLAY ZONE

When author and mother Liz Curtis Higgs asked older moms what they wish they'd done differently as mothers of young children, they said they wished for "more . . . fun, hugs, time, reading, playing, listening, accessibility, kisses, positive reinforcement . . ."[11]

Sometimes as moms we need a jump-start to enter the Play Zone. We need some guidelines that help motivate us to give our children Play-With-Me Love. Here are some tips to get you started.

Be Spontaneous

Lighten up and seize upon opportunities to be spontaneous. Nancie Carmichael, co-founder with her husband, Bill, of *Virtue* and *Christian Parenting Today* magazines, remembers some spontaneous, fun family times: "One day just before the school bus came by to bring the kids home, our dog, Chester (the ugliest dog you ever saw), was at my feet while I was folding laundry. Chester always went out to meet the kids. I had a pair of Andy's Superman Underoos in my hand and thought, *Why not?* So I put them on Chester and sent him out to meet the kids. The gales of laughter from the boys at the sight of Chester were worth it."[12]

Surprise your child by playing hooky from your regular routines for one whole day. Wear your clothes inside out and see if anyone notices. Eat dessert first. Wake your child up to search for shooting stars in the night sky. Be spontaneous and watch fun develop!

Find the "Extra" in the Ordinary

You can enter the Play Zone in the most mundane moments of life—if you're looking for it! In this poem entitled "My Mom Took Us Out In The Rain," one mom from Arizona describes the "extra" she found in an ordinary moment when she chose to enter into it gleefully.

"My mom took us out in the rain!"
They'll remember again and again,
When their memory gears to their childhood years—
"My mom took us out in the rain!"

Now, you may think rain is a bore,
If it visits you over and o're.
But to us it's a treat,
And the sound is so sweet
When it touches our dry desert floor.

But my neighbors—it's actually true!—
Go about as if nothing were new.
they sit in their houses
As quiet as mouses,
And watch that big box that is blue.

But the minute a drop of it comes,
Our house with activity hums.
Grab a towel or two
And some boots or old shoes,
It mightn't last long, so we run!

Umbrellas? We have none and will
Never need them, our dream to fulfill.
Have you figured it yet?
Our goals's to get wet!
And attain it we certainly will.

I imagine the neighbors are huddled
In front of their windows, befuddled.
"Have you seen," they must say,
"How she lets her kids lay
With their tummies flat down in a puddle?"

And I do, while I watch with a grin,
As it undulates under their chin.
"For what good" I explain,
"Is a walk in the rain,
If you don't come home soaked to the skin?"

As for me, I am wet as a hen.
Not the prettiest I've ever been.
Howe'er I surmise,
That when seen through their eyes,
That to them I am beautiful then.

And after, the porch by our door,
Is strewn with wet clothing galore.
Inside warm and snug,
We share blankets and hugs,
Our memories richer the more.

A walk in the rain is not new.
And it takes just a minute or two.
But your children will know,
As they watch and they grow,
That they were important to you.

"My mom took us out in the rain!"
From their lips let me hear that refrain.
"My mom took us out in the rain!"
And I hope that someday,
their own children will say,
"My mom took us out in the rain!"[13]

Carole Wright

Playing helps lighten my spirit. Mealtimes are great for lighthearted, fun conversation. Our children also really like it when my husband and I are playful with each other!

— ❧ —

Isn't that great? Can you put the "extra" in the ordinary? Try it. Put chocolate chip happy faces in your Saturday morning pancakes. Splash big and hard in the bathtub. Stay up late together and watch a goofy movie and eat popcorn. Find the something special in the everyday ordinariness and play in it.

Laugh

When's the last time you really hooted and hollered with your little ones? Joining into their giggly, funny laughter is pure fun! Here's what pastor and author Walt Wangerin says in *Little Lamb, Who Made Thee?* about children, play, and laughter:

> Let the children laugh and be glad.
>
> O my dear, they haven't long before the world assaults them. Allow them genuine laughter now. Laugh with them, till tears run down your faces—till a memory of pure delight and precious relationship is established within them, indestructible, personal and forever. Soon enough they'll meet faces unreasonably enraged. Soon enough they'll be accused of things they did not do. So give your children . . . golden days, their own pure days, in which they are so clearly and dearly beloved that they believe in love and in their own particular worth when love shall seem in short supply hereafter. Give them laughter. . . . Because the laughter that is so easy in childhood must echo its encouragement a long, long time. A lifetime.[14]

Laugh often and heartily. Help your children keep their giggles going. Play Simon Says, Crazy Eights, Twister, Head-Shoulders-

Knees-and-Toes. Do the Hokey Pokey. Hum with a kazoo. Put some silly-willies into your day, and let them take you to the floor in laughter.

My four-year-old called me from my neighbor's house just to "talk," and then out of the blue she asked, "Mommy, how do you laugh?" and I suddenly realized that I don't very often.

— ❧ —

As you laugh, be mindful of the subtle differences between laughing *at* our children and laughing *with* them. Do you know these differences? Karen Dockrey points some out for us. For instance, recall the funny things your children did in a way that makes them feel treasured rather than shamed or ridiculed. When we laugh *with* our kids, we empower and encourage them in play but when we laugh *at* them, they feel embarrassed, weakened, and at times, even stupid.[15]

Laugh together at something they find funny. When they make a joke, giggle along, no matter how silly it may seem. Also, learn to laugh at your own mistakes and invite your children to join in! Let laughter lead you in play and enjoy where it takes you!

We try to write down funny things our kids say, like this recent prayer from our four-year-old: "Dear Lord, thank you for today. Help me and Steph and Mom have a good sleep. Thanks for already helping Dad to sleep on the couch."

— ❧ —

Provide Toys

Children don't need elaborate or expensive toys, but toys can be the tools to motivate play and fun. Miriam Huffman Rockness in *A Time to Play* encourages parents to stock their "children's 'workshop'" with a wide variety of tools to make possible a wide range of experiences. These should include: recreational equipment, tools for exploring the world of nature, water gear,

Sometimes we have a bubble gum blowing contest or think of all the games we can play with balloons.

— ❧ —

games and puzzles, art supplies, musical instruments, books, records, and props for making believe."[16]

Turn the Negatives into Positives

Fun comes when we learn to lighten up and turn negatives into positives. How can you do this as you raise your children?

Never say no if you can say yes

Bite your tongue down on the word no. Say it only when absolutely necessary. Of course you can't say yes to every request, but when you can find a compromise or positive alternative, do it with gusto.

Turn disasters into fun

Pastor and author Tom Eisenman writes of a time when his mom turned a disaster into fun on the farm he grew up on in Wisconsin:

"The farmhouse had a huge kitchen with a linoleum floor. One modern convenience in the kitchen was a dishwasher. One summer afternoon the dishwasher exploded, and water and suds shot out all over the kitchen. The kitchen floor was transformed into a lake of hot, soapy water.

My daughter was having a "downer day" and came to me with her whole face smeared with bright red lipstick. She knew she was not supposed to be in my make-up. But instead of being mad at that moment, we laughed together.

— ❧ —

"My mom yelled, 'Get your swimming suits!' For the next hour we took turns running through the living room, diving into the kitchen and sliding across the soapy kitchen floor. We had the time of our lives. My mom told all of her friends how great it was not to have to scrub that week."[17]

Think positively

Attitude is everything, and a positive attitude is not only contagious, it breeds a sense of fun. Research also shows a positive attitude is good for your health. So twist the negative into a positive with affirming words. For instance, when you and your child are soaked to the skin by a sudden thundershower as you are walking across a parking lot, consider your response. You could grumble and complain about being miserably wet, or turn the experience into an adventure by imagining the great stories you'll tell about the walk in the rain.

When you next face the gripes, give them a positive twist.

Plan to Play

If you're not a spontaneous person, but need to put more play in your child's life, you can resort to one last option: plan your play. Choose from this list of play suggestions and add your own.

Hold a no-silverware dinner

Forget most of your family's normal manners like saying "please" and "thank you." Eat with your fingers. Blow bubbles in your milk. All talk at once. Chew with your mouths open. Enforce only one rule: no throwing food. (Although you could if you're outside!)

Stage an indoor picnic

Spread a blanket out in the middle of the living room. Eat fried chicken and potato salad.

We used to have "bathtub picnics." I prepared a tray with little bowls of pineapple, macaroni and cheese, or baked beans and put the tray in the bathroom. I put the kids in the tub, fed them dinner, and washed them up (easy cleanup!). Any small pieces of food that went down the drain, well, they were "for the fish!"

— 🙢 —

Play Nerf volleyball and do a three-legged race. Don't forget the sunscreen!

Have a red dinner for Valentine's Day

Serve spaghetti with red sauce, red jello, watermelon, strawberries, and anything else red that comes to mind. Hold a staring contest and see whose face turns the reddest, or share your most embarrassing moment. Eat toast with red jam and Kool-Aid, and tell each other one thing you really like about each other.

Live backwards for one evening

Sometimes I force myself to put music on and sing—loud—and dance. I also take a moment to play jacks or go down the slide at the playground. I try to stop and see the world from the child's perspective ... even the vacuum cleaner is fun to ride on!

— ❧ —

Begin with bedtime stories and hugs and kisses. Get in your pajamas and then eat dinner. Dessert first, of course, before the main dish.

Hold a family meeting, and add your own ideas to this list. Plan to create fun.

GETTING TO THE HEART
OF PLAY-WITH-ME LOVE

Children need to have fun. They need to develop their creativity and use their imagination to explore the world and their own potential. As moms, we can squelch or encourage this need by our attitude and willingness. Though we can't always drop everything and build blanket forts or snowpeople or blow bubbles or fly kites with our children all the time, we can drop everything some of the time. We can provide playful tools or toys for our children. We can encourage them to be children and acknowledge the importance of play as a child's work. We can show love to our children by recognizing and meeting their need for Play-With-Me Love.

Love Handles

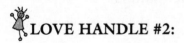 **LOVE HANDLE #1:**

Helping Babies Learn Through Play

Reaching out (0–6 months)

Attract your baby's attention with something colorful that makes a noise. She'll show her interest by wriggling and throwing her limbs out, clumsily trying to grab it.

Ball control (6–12 months)

Your baby will be fascinated to see a ball rolling around but surprised when she accidentally makes it move. By a year, she'll be able to pick it up, throw it, and roll it.

Making noises (6–12 months)

A wooden spoon and saucepan make a perfect drum. Your baby will love banging away and listening to the loud noise.

New sensations (6–12 months)

Show your baby how water behaves and feels on her hands. Plastic cups make good substitutes for toy buckets.[18]

LOVE HANDLE #2:

Encouraging Playtime

How do we encourage our children to play and jump-start their creativity? Here are some suggestions:

- Encourage their imagination. Don't feel they always have to be learning or "accomplishing" something. Let them create their own play. Resist the urge to schedule their play. Let them figure it out. And don't be afraid of the phrase "I'm bored." Boredom often forces kids to create things to do.

- Provide creative materials. You don't have to purchase "educational" toys. Just look around your home. You'll be amazed at what you'll find, such as paper and crayons, buttons and scrap material, and small cartons. And don't forget nature's toys, such as rocks, shells, or feathers.

- Make exercise fun. Jumping rope and jumping jacks to music are two fun exercises. Children can also create their own Olympics or triathalons. Exercising can be fun, and learning that now helps children grow up to be healthy adults.

- Suggest a business. Try vegetable stands, garage sales, trading baseball cards, or a neighborhood circus.

- Play with them. Get down on your hands and knees and introduce them to new games and activities.

- Tolerate the creative chaos. Try to relax and remember that we are guiding our children with information and support during these years.[19]

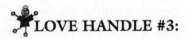 LOVE HANDLE #3:

Growing Creative Children

Here are some ways to nurture your child's creative potential:

- Be a creative mom. Let your child see that you enjoy creative activities and new projects, like needlepoint or hanging wallpaper or decorating cakes or black and white photography. Your creative quest is contagious. Your child is an imitator.

- Play "what if" games. What if you could fly? Where would you go? What if our dog Barney could talk?

What would he say? What if we had no TVs in the world? What would people do? What if you were the mommy, and I was the little boy?

- Make up your own stories. Let your children make up their own stories. Let one person name three main objects and the other person make up a story using them, such as a bunny rabbit, a space rocket, and a magic watch.
- Create or allow unstructured time. Don't overschedule children in activities. Be sure they experience "down" time to let their minds wander or to learn to enjoy their own company. Keep naptime a quiet time, even after they outgrow naps.
- Help them to see beyond the mundane. Go on a hike and look for animal shapes in clouds or faces in rock formations. Appreciate the intricacies of a ladybug or a pinecone. Help them see the wonder of nature in a flower or a bird.
- Introduce your children to new situations and to people who don't look or act just the way they do. Children grow as they are exposed to the unfamiliar. Invite a non-English speaking family to dinner. Get to know a hearing impaired person and some sign language.
- Encourage your children to collect something. Rocks. Baseball cards. Unusual dolls. Stamps. Coins. Postcards. Ball caps.

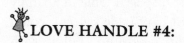

LOVE HANDLE #4:

Choosing the Right Toys

- Choose toys that allow a child to use imagination. Don't buy toys that do everything and therefore leave little room for a child to fill in the missing details, such as toys with recorded messages that direct all their play.

- Purchase toys expecting that your child will play with them vigorously. Don't buy an expensive teddy bear and get upset if your child washes its face. As *The Velveteen Rabbit* teaches us, well-used toys are the best loved.

- Buy toys that have more than one use. Toys meant for building, such as blocks and Legos, can be used for making structures but also for housing plastic figures and animals. Children like to mix and match toys.

- Choose toys that are safe and age-appropriate. Some unusual examples include:

    Two-year-olds: hand puppets, box of costumes, children's tape recorder.

    Three-year-olds: window bird feeder and bird guide, suitcases, finger paints.

    Four-year-olds: flashlight, magnifying glass, preschool computer software.

    Five-year-olds: jigsaw puzzles, kites, deck of cards.

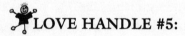LOVE HANDLE #5:

"Imagination Station"

Why not put together an "Imagination Station" for your child? If you have room, it could be a special table in a family room or kitchen corner. If you don't have table space, it could be a box of supplies that you move around. Fill it with creativity-inspiring supplies, such as crayons, chalk, blank paper, stamps, stickers, coloring books, construction paper, scissors (the kids' kind), glue, pipe cleaners, paper clips, watercolors, finger paints, clay or Play-Doh, origami books, or puzzles.

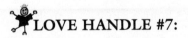

LOVE HANDLE #6:

Books Are Fun!

Think of the ways you can use books.

- Read aloud.
- Act out the stories. Change your voice for each character. Use hand gestures.
- Ask questions as you read. "Guess what's going to happen?" "What do you see?" "What is going on here?"
- Record your child's favorite book so she can play it back anytime.
- Read in bed. Read in the car. Read on a hammock. Read while waiting in the doctor's office.
- As soon as your child is old enough to enjoy looking at books, get him his own book light for reading in bed.
- Purchase an inexpensive bookshelf so your child can keep his books together in his own "library."
- Visit the library often for checking out books and for story time. Obtain a library card for your child that she can use herself.

LOVE HANDLE #7:

Fun During Chores

Turn chores into fun with these simple suggestions:

- Music to Clean By: Play your child's favorite music and dub it "cleanup music."
- Here's Why: Challenge your children to find the reason for every job that needs doing, and what's good about

doing it. Have a contest to see who can think of the most reasons.

- As-You's: Cut down on chores by having everyone participate in As-You's. Everyone carries his own dirty clothes to the hamper As-You change. Everyone carries her own dishes to the sink As-You finish eating. Everybody wipes his feet As-You enter the house.
- A Better Way: Have a discussion about some of the regular chores and take suggestions about how they could be done better.
- Clock Check: Race against the clock to complete particularly tedious chores. Set the timer on the stove or microwave. Other times, try racing against each other to make everyone's chores more fun.
- Reward at the End: Use chore charts for young children. Let them add a sticker each time they finish a chore. Filling in all the stickers in a row means a reward, like an ice-cream cone or movie, or whatever you've determined.[20]

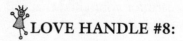**LOVE HANDLE #8:**

Car Fun

Have fun while riding in a car. The trip can be as much fun as the destination.

- The Alphabet Game: Starting with "A," find something out the window that starts with each letter of the alphabet.
- Dimes on the Dashboard: This virtually eliminates car bickering. Display a stack of ten dimes on the dashboard for each child. Explain that you'll take away a dime every time they say an unkind word or show an uncooperative attitude. At the end of each one hundred

miles, they can keep whatever dimes are left and start with ten new dimes.

- Mind-Spin: Take turns saying the first word that pops in your mind with each member in the car. "Spotted." "Owl." "Bunny." "Easter." "Eggs." "Scrambled." And so on.
- Top-of-the Hour Fun: Pack a new activity for each hour on the road. Possibilities include new books, music tapes, small travel games, or special snacks.[21]

MOM READING:

The Big Book of Family Fun, Claudia Arp and Linda Dillow
Creative, Confident Children, Maxine Hancock
Family Celebrations at Birthdays, Ann Hibbard
The Family Manager, Kathy Peel
Help! I'm Being Intimidated by the Proverbs 31 Woman! Nancy
   Kennedy
Honey for A Child's Heart, Gladys Hunt
The Hurried Child, David Elkind

LAP READING:

Amelia Bedelia, Peggy Parish
Finger Rhymes and *Hand Rhymes,* Marc Brown
Oh, Were They Ever Happy! Peter Spier
Shake My Sillies Out, Raffi: Songs to Read
The Snowy Day, Ezra Jack Keats
The Tale of Peter Rabbit, Beatrix Potter
We're Going on a Bear Hunt, Michael Rosen
Winnie the Pooh, A. A. Milne

Independence:
Let-Me-Grow-Up Love

Jeannie considered her five-year-old son's request. Could Matthew walk down to his friend's house all by himself?

The friend lived only about a block away, but their house was around the corner, and Jeannie couldn't watch her son go the whole way. In the simple question before her, somehow Jeannie knew that more was at stake than just a trip around the corner. This was a growing-up decision. Was her son ready? Was Jeannie ready?

Mentally paging back through the last weeks, Jeannie knew they'd been preparing for this moment. They'd taken it in stages. First she'd walked Matthew the whole way, and then just to the corner. There Jeannie stood like a sentry, protectively watching her son's little legs propel him the remaining distance, up the steps, and to the front door. Only when Matthew was safely inside was Jeannie able to turn and make her way back up the street to home. Was her son ready to make this trip alone?

"Okay, Matthew, here's the deal," Jeannie concluded. "You may walk to Josh's, but you *must* call me the *minute* you get inside to let me know that you made it. Okay?"

"Sure, Mom!" Matthew attached his mother's permission to himself like a parachute and launched through their front door, down the steps, and into the outside world.

"Remember, Matthew, call me as *soon* as you get there!" Jeannie yelled after him.

"Okay, Mom!" Matthew promised, with just a hint of impatience in his voice, as he started running down the sidewalk. He didn't even turn around to look back at his mother, who now stood, hands on her hips, on the porch.

Jeannie made herself go back into the house, but then she walked straight to the upstairs window that had the best view down the street. There she could see Matthew, a small figure alone on a big street. He reached the corner, paused, then turned and disappeared from sight.

Jeannie sat down on her bed by the phone and had a mental flash of watching a "splash down" years ago when astronauts reentered the earth's atmosphere. For a dreadful few minutes, all contact was lost with NASA's Command Central. Something could have gone terribly wrong with the astronauts, and the engineers wouldn't have known it. Why did she think about such things at a time like this? Why did she suddenly remember all the grim stories she'd ever heard about children being snatched from street corners or backyards? So many frightening possibilities lurked in the world out there.

How silly! she scolded herself. Matthew would be fine! He needed this kind of freedom and independence if he was ever going to grow up and make it on his own in life!

But he should be calling by now, Jeannie thought as she looked at the phone. Maybe she should call. No, Matthew needed to remember on his own. If Jeannie called, she'd be undoing everything and thwarting her son's need for some Let-Me-Grow-Up Love. She'd give him a few more minutes.

Jeannie walked briskly down the hall to Matthew's room. There she spied a stray sock peeping out from underneath the bed, stooped to retrieve it, and found herself locked in a stare with Jumpy, Matthew's stuffed kangaroo pal. "We're going to miss him, Jumpy, aren't we? I can already feel the hole he'll leave in my heart when he takes off for good. But sometimes I wonder how much independence he can handle. Do I give him too much, Jumpy? Or not enough?"

Jeannie tenderly smoothed her son's bed pillows and set Jumpy straight in his place. Why couldn't she let go of the doubts swirling in her head?

Down the hall in her bedroom, the phone rang.

A CHILD'S NEED FOR INDEPENDENCE

Every child needs independence. In order to grow and become a healthy, fully functioning adult, children need to learn to operate within a scope of freedom where choices are independently made and consequences experienced.

Independence is built on the foundation of discipline and respect. As discipline and respect provide roots, independence gives wings. Limits and space. Security and freedom. Beginning with the exit of a baby from his mother's womb, this Let-Me-Grow-Up Love launches a child out into a world to live as a whole, healthy, free individual in his own right.

Drs. Henry Cloud and John Townsend write in *Boundaries* that "as infants gain a sense of internal safety and attachment, [another] need arises. The baby's need for autonomy, or independence, starts to emerge. Child experts call this *separation* and *individuation*. 'Separation' refers to the child's need to perceive him or herself as distinct from Mother, a 'not-me' experience. 'Individuation' describes the identity the child develops while separating from Mother. It's a 'me' experience."[1]

Independence is one of the toughest needs for a mom to meet in her child. Let-Me-Grow-Up Love is the child's natural need for independence. It is a process with a purpose. When we understand the normality of the need and its purpose, we've taken a giant step in providing for this need in our child.

Independence Is a Process

Independence isn't given in a one-time dose. Rather, it is a complicated, continuing challenge for parents. As explained in *Learning to Let Go,* "independence is not a single event that happens the day a child leaves home for college, an apartment, marriage, or a job. Rather it is a slow, physical and emotional process that starts the moment the umbilical cord is cut at birth and continues in little bits and pieces, moment by moment, as a child grows up. It is a process with specific goals, characteristics, and a logical, predictable order of events."[2]

The goals of letting go are twofold: to prepare the child for independence from the parents and to prepare the parents for life without the child.

Our children start off in the boat of life with us as their guide. Soon they are sitting in their own little dinghy attached alongside our boat, still under our control and direction. Little by little, we let out the rope so that, while still connected, they start to get the feeling of being apart and begin to make some decisions in controlling their own boat.

— ❧ —

In most families, Let-Me-Grow-Up Love is a gradual gift, given in stages over a long period of time. First, a child chooses between two outfits to wear. Then she selects her own outfits. Then she washes and folds her outfits. Finally, she buys her outfits.

First, a child is taught to take his cup and plate to the sink. Then he learns to rinse it off. Then he loads and unloads the dishwasher. Finally, he cleans up after himself without being told.

Independence Is a Process with a Purpose

We raise our children to leave us. Does that sentence cause a twinge of regret or surprise in your heart? It is poignant and even painful, but the goal of mothering is to allow and encourage a child to experience the freedom of independence. Someone once said, "Mothers were not meant for leaning upon. Mothers were meant to make leaning unnecessary." Another wise someone commented, "A mother's lap is meant to be a launching pad for life." Both reflections show the process starts with holding on and moves toward letting go.

What is your goal in mothering? Defining your goal now will help you to make good choices as you offer Let-Me-Grow-Up Love to your children in the days, months, and years to come.

Independence Is a Process with a Purpose that Teaches Life-Lessons

Life-lessons are truths learned by trial and error. The true equipping for life that children need to survive and thrive on their own often comes only through freedom in independence.

Life-lesson #1: Identity

Identity is our understanding of who we are—who we were created to be—as unique individuals. Developmental psychologists believe that a child begins his life with a need to bond with his mother and actually sees her as an extension of himself. Her breast responds to his cries of hunger and meets his need for food. Her arms serve as his own room/bed/womb of comfort.

Just as a baby has a need to bond, he also has a need to eventually separate and recognize his separate identity from his mother. A son does not need to hold his mother's hand as he goes off to middle school. A daughter does not need to cling to her mother's legs when she feels afraid as she enters high school. And when a child is given the freedom to choose and to be, that child learns the life-lesson of identity as a separate and capable individual.

Life-lesson #2: Responsibility

If we spell the word *responsibility* a bit differently, we can see the meaning behind the letters. It's more like "response-ability" or the ability to respond. In *The Book of Virtues*, William J. Bennett writes, "Responsible persons are mature people who have taken charge of themselves and their conduct, who own their actions and own up to them—who answer for them."[3]

Independence fosters responsibility and vice versa. Abigail Van Buren ("Dear Abby") observed, "If you want your children to keep their feet on the ground, put some responsibility on their shoulders."[4] In other words, help them to strengthen their ability to respond to life on their own. Don't solve all their problems for them. When your daughter asks you where her shoe is, challenge her to answer her own question. "If you were the mommy, how would you answer that question?"

Freedom in making decisions about how to spend a two-dollar allowance, or what to select from a restaurant menu, or what to wear on a Saturday morning, or how to keep a bedroom clean—such tasks layer learning in the life of a child. When independence is given, responsibility is learned. When children shoulder responsibilities they gain confidence and experience independence.

Life-lesson #3: Self-discipline

The purpose of discipline and limits is to lead to self-discipline. Independence means self-discipline. It moves a child from being told what to do, to being able to do on his own. It brings the external boundaries inside the child, internalizing a standard for choice-making. Independence helps a child learn that the person in charge of me is *me*!

You've seen it happen. You teach your three-year-old to "listen to his tummy" when deciding whether he wants seconds at dinner. Suddenly he's six. You're out to dinner, and the waitress asks if he'd like another cola. He pauses, considers, and announces that his mouth wants another, but his tummy doesn't.

A simple lesson like learning to make a bed before playing in the morning translates into doing homework before watching TV, at the child's initiative. The careful saving of quarters for weeks to purchase an outfit for a doll translates into the putting aside of funds for a new sweater that didn't fit into the clothing budget.

Clarify your standards when teaching self-discipline. "Clearing the table means taking the dishes to the sink and wiping off the table." Ask children to redo it right, if the result is not adequate (taking into account the age-appropriate result.) "Clearing the table means taking *all* the dishes to the sink and wiping the whole table." Establish deadlines for tasks. These kinds of limits and guidance help to build the sense of self-discipline.

Independence teaches the life-lesson of self-discipline. It moves a child from listening to a mother tell him what to do, to doing for himself.

Life-lesson #4: Self-confidence

As a bonus to identity, responsibility, and self-discipline, independence also teaches the life-lesson of self-confidence.

Try sending your eight-year-old into the grocery store for one item with the correct amount of money while you wait in the car. Before she goes in, remember together where in the store the item is located and review the steps for

My daughter was four when she came up to me and said, "Mom, look at me, but don't see!" She wanted me to be there for her, but not to judge what she was doing. (As it turned out, it wasn't a life-threatening activity . . . just a little sneaky!) Children need the security of mom's love but also the room to experiment and grow.

— ❧ —

purchasing. Then don't spy. Don't hover. Wait. Give her the freedom of independence to try the task on her own.

Confidence is the most difficult thing for me to instill in my children, partly because I lack confidence in myself and partly because it's hard for me to give up my way. Too often I find myself resetting the table or refolding the laundry after they have done it.

— ❧ —

When she emerges, beaming with success, praise her, and then pat yourself on the back. In her journey toward independence, you've just given her the opportunity to learn the life-lesson of self-confidence.

From this success, she will take another risk, then another, and then another.

What a great gift to give our children! To understand their limits and abilities—and to live within them—builds confidence!

Life-lesson #5: Interdependence

Independence should teach the lesson of appropriate interdependence. We are meant to live in relationships with others in meaningful ways. As we help our children learn to be independent and capable, we also teach them when to ask for help. They need to learn when to depend upon others in appropriate ways. The best way to teach this tricky lesson is to model it.

Mom to Mom illustrates the need for interdependence with a story of a mom with the flu who doesn't want to ask anyone for help.

Why? I picked up one excuse after another, examining its offerings. *I don't want to bother anyone.* After all, other women had their own children and schedules to keep.

But to be honest, I knew that wasn't the real reason. *I don't want to owe anyone.* How would I ever repay their kindness? That was closer, but it still wasn't the core.

Ah. Here it is. The real reason: *I'm not supposed to need any-body. I'm supposed to do this myself and by myself. If I can't do this by myself, there must be something wrong with me.*[5]

We want to discover our own sometimes mixed-up attitudes about independence and interdependence and help our children learn about appropriate interdependence.

Independence is a process with a purpose that teaches life-lessons. Randolph Sanders observes that "the child whose parents give him a balance of limits and independence learns to be secure in the knowledge that his parents will intervene when he gets too far out on a limb. These children learn that pushing forward can be harmful when it hurts you or other people. They learn that venturing ahead can be wonderful when it leads to discovery, invention, and fulfillment. Over time, they learn how to use their own judgment to decide when to push forward into unchartered territory and when not.[6]

LET-ME-GROW-UP LOVE
IS DIFFICULT TO GIVE

As we said earlier, a child's need for independence may be the most difficult need for mothers to meet because we run into some major mom-bumps along the way! Giving independence often conflicts with a mother's instinct to protect her child. Knowing when to hold on and when to let go is tricky. It's like running alongside a five-year-old who is learning to ride a two-wheeler. We grab the back of the seat to hold it upright, lunging for the handlebars when it tips. We *so* much want the child to get his own balance and go for it. At the same time, we know that letting go might put him at risk. But holding on too long puts both of us at risk. The dilemma creates a mother's conflict of head and heart, of risk and security.

Mom's Needs

Several of our own needs get in the way and stall our progress in meeting our children's need for Let-Me-Grow-Up Love. Some needs may apply to you while others may not.

"I need to know I'm okay as a mom."

Every mom is different. You may have *loved* the infant stage, but you're having trouble handling your two-year-old's quest for independence, and you can't understand how your sister can *love* the teenage years. How can she so readily celebrate her son getting his driver's license? You look ahead to your five-year-old heading off to kindergarten next fall and your throat tightens with emotion. Or you listen to friends who worry about their middle-schoolers going off to the mall—alone! You look at your own preteens and rejoice in all they are learning, and celebrate each step of independence they take away from you. You don't understand your friends' reluctance.

It is difficult to draw that fine line between loving and nurturing my children and smothering and overprotecting them. I'm constantly trying to keep that balance in check, which becomes difficult because it's a constant questioning of my mothering ability.

— ❧ —

If you tend to compare yourself to other moms who are different, stop. You are you. "Different" doesn't mean wrong.

"I need my child to stay the same because I don't like change!"

Letting go is a process based on changing the way we show our love to our children, so Let-Me-Grow-Up Love is laced with change. We can't express our love to a ten-year-old the same way we did when she was ten months old. Nor can we successfully offer the same kind of love to a nineteen-year-old that we offered a ten-year-old.

A mother needs to change the way she expresses her love as a child grows. "Love crawls with the baby, walks with the toddler, runs with the child, then stands aside to let the youth walk into

> *The most difficult part of parenting is adjusting and knowing when to make the necessary changes in guidelines and rules as they grow older. Releasing them slowly, giving them more responsibility, and trusting them can be difficult at times.*
>
> — ❧ —

adulthood."[7] In the beginning, we love by protecting and limiting. Later on, we love by pulling back and letting go.

As moms, we also need to allow our children to change the way they show their love for us. In the first year of life a mother is adored by a child, but as a child approaches the second birthday, she has a growing need for separation and a greater need for the world beyond mother. "Many mothers find this transition from their child's love affair with them to the big wide world difficult," say Drs. Henry Cloud and John Townsend in *Boundaries*. "The loss of such a deep intimacy is great, especially after the time spent in pregnancy and childbirth. The responsible mother, however, will strive to get her own closeness needs met by other adults in her life."[8]

The mom who has a difficult time adjusting to change may have a difficult time meeting her child's need for independence.

"I need to be needed. Being a mom is an important part of who I am."

When children start showing signs of independence, some moms panic. We may suddenly realize that our children will not always be around to provide an identity for us. Test yourself by considering these questions:

- Who am I if my child doesn't need me anymore?
- Who am I if my child doesn't perform successfully?

- Who am I if my child disappoints me?
- Who am I if my child is different from what I expected?
- Who am I if my child leaves home?

All of these questions convey changes in relationships. But even deeper within each is the experience of loss. The external definition of who we are shifts when our children grow and go away from us. We seek new identities and grieve the loss of old ones. We experience this loss when a baby weans from the breast or bottle, teeters in her first steps, walks down to a friend's house to play, gets on the school bus for the day, drives away in a car without us, or packs up her bedroom for college.

When my five-year-old went to her first day of preschool at age two, I was reluctant to leave her. She said, "Go home and fix your hair." In other words, "I'll be okay, Mommy. Trust me."

— ❧ —

In such moments, we need to remind ourselves that our worth and value doesn't come from our role as mothers. Just as we were able to shift from a teenager to an adult focus, from a single to a married focus, or from a career to a mother focus, we can make this shift from mother focus to other focus; from holding on to letting go.

"I need to not worry about my child."

Sometimes we just want to keep our children at home where we assume they are safe. We fear that sending them off will put them at risk. We presume that as long as our children are under our own roofs, we can control what goes into their mouths and their heads and their ears. We can keep track of what they are doing. We won't worry as much. Life will be so much easier.

"How many mistakes I have made with the children because I was fretting," says Ruth Bell Graham, "concerned to the point of worry. And invariably it prompted me to unwise action:

sharpness, unfair punishment, unwise discipline. But a mother who walks with God knows he only asks her to take care of the possible and to trust him with the impossible; she does not need to fret."[9]

The mom-bump of worry is completely counteracted only through faith. If we truly believe that we alone are responsible for the life of our child, we will paralyze ourselves with a lifetime of worry. If, however, we see mothering as a partnership with an all-powerful God who is ultimately responsible for our child and utterly able to care for our child, then we have hope.

Poet Susan Lenzkes expresses this realization in a poem aptly titled "Trust."

> Stoop-shouldered,
> foot-dragging,
> sighing
> resignation
> is not trust.
>
> Real trust
> bounces on eager toes of
> anticipation—
> laughs with the pure delight
> of knowing
> in whom it believes—
> rests easy
> knowing
> on whom it waits.
>
> Lord,
> so wrap me in the
> knowledge of You
> that my trust is no longer
> in You, but
> is You.[10]

Similarly, Bible scholar A.W. Tozer offers trust as a remedy for the mom-bump of worry. "We are often hindered from giving up our treasures to the Lord out of fear for their safety; this is especially true when those treasures are loved relatives and friends. But we need have no such fears. Our Lord does not come to destroy but to save. Everything is safe which we commit to Him, and nothing is really safe which is not so committed."[11]

"I need to protect my child from suffering."

How can we stand by and watch our children struggle? How can we allow our children to make mistakes or fail, when we can help or prevent that pain? For many moms, this is a painful challenge.

These words from *A Mother's Footprints of Faith* say it so well: " ... I want to protect myself from the pain of watching and waiting while my kids discover the lesson tucked into the struggle. While the baby cries himself to sleep. While the toddler keeps falling down when learning to walk. While the preschooler struggles to find an appropriate response to another child who won't share any toys. I am, at times, tempted to rush in and rescue my children with a quick-fix solution."[12]

It's hard for me to let my children make questionable choices. Sometimes I get impatient because it seems like they aren't "learning their lesson" when a choice they made isn't satisfactory. For example, my six-year-old daughter always chooses to spend her allowance on candy or gum. Therefore, she doesn't have money for a toy or something else that she wants.

— ❧ —

Such sentiments echo with stirrings in most mother hearts. Ah—if we could but fix the circumstances in the lives of our children, we could ensure their success and happiness.

But while the quick-fix solution feels good to us, it's not always the best solution for our children. In fact, the quick fix can come between our children and their growth toward independence. Our rescuing and protecting can subtly *teach* our children that they cannot handle life alone. And this is exactly the opposite of what they need.

Children learn to walk by falling down and getting back up again. They learn to read by struggling through nonsensical syllables.

> *Sometimes my own fear of my children failing or getting hurt stops me from letting them try something new.*
>
> — ❧ —

They learn to choose well by choosing badly. The most vivid memories are accompanied by the strongest feelings. No wonder the greatest laboratory of life is the laboratory of error, and this pattern—of making mistakes, learning a lesson, and moving on—is best to begin when children are young.

When you bump into your own need to protect your child, remind yourself that your goal is not to fix the world for your child, but to fix your child to be able to live and cope in the world. This comes by offering some Let-Me-Grow-Up Love.

Mom's Challenge

We can easily get our emotions and agendas tangled up in the process of meeting the needs of our children. Which need is most important when? Does she need security or independence? Affirmation or discipline? And what on earth is going on inside me as a mom in this process? Several realizations help us untangle our emotions from this process.

Understand your vital role as a mom

Moms are essential in the process of both growing and going. As vital as it is for moms to attach to their babies and for their babies to attach to their moms, it is equally important for the mom to encourage independence and allow her child to decrease dependence upon her. "After providing a close nurturing relationship," Drs. Henry Cloud and John Townsend say, "it is the mother's responsibility to assist her child in becoming an individual. In order to do this, Mom needs some skills. She must: 1. foster independence and assertion of will, intentionality, and separateness. 2. foster individual identity and differences."[13]

You must nudge your child's going. You must allow her to become dependent upon others; her father, a trusted babysitter, or friends. The truth is, a mother can't meet all her child's needs all the time.

Family expert Ron Hutchcraft uses an illustration from nature to underline the mother's role in a child's independence.

> My friends from eagle country tell me that [the mother eagle] realizes her babies need a little help venturing out of the nest. So when the eaglets are getting old enough to learn to fly, Mother Eagle starts to "uncomfort" the nest. She starts to put sharp sticks and stones inside so Baby Eagle will be motivated to get out and soar. The result is majestic.

> Mother Eagle's lesson? "If your kids are ever going to fly, you need to be an ally of their freedom." Unfortunately, many children get the impression that they have to fight their mother and father to get out of the nest![14]

Consider the alternative

A mother's challenge to offer independence is much easier to handle when we consider the result of not meeting this need. Do you really want to raise a child who is emotionally paralyzed with dependence, who clings to your leg, or has no confidence and never leaves home?

Of course not! Mom bumps are smoothed out when we look past where we are in this moment to where we want our children to be in the future. Considering the alternative to independence provides a reality check that helps us to loosen our grip and slowly let go.

HOW TO GIVE LET-ME-GROW-UP LOVE

Remember, independence is a process with a purpose. When a child is born, that child is one hundred percent dependent upon us and gradually moves to independence from us and healthy interdependence on others. It doesn't happen all at once, but rather is given out in increasing doses.

As you respond to your child's need for Let-Me-Grow-Up love, keep the following guidelines in mind.

Practice Freedom-Giving

"Even when they are little," Ron Hutchcraft says, "children should be given little freedom practices—privileges that grow as they show they can be trusted. This trustworthiness freedom cycle is parenting at its best—practically preparing your child to live without you."[15]

As we said in the last chapter on the need for Give-Me-Limits Love, clarify the rules, consequences, and limits, and each year move to increased freedom in a slow, orderly process. Instead of tightening your grip on your child, you'll actually want to work hard to loosen it with freedom practices.

Each year, for instance, a child should be given more freedom about going to a friend's house in the neighborhood. First, a mother goes with him and stays while the friends play. Then, she walks him over, teaching him about cars and crossings and strangers. Then, she allows him to walk by himself, insisting that he call home when he gets there. Finally, he is old enough to spend the night with his friend. This gradual process teaches him to make good choices and gain confidence in his ability to cope with growing independence.

Teach How to Think, Not What to Think

There's an old saying that goes, "Give a man a fish, feed him for a day. Teach a man to fish, feed him for a lifetime." Independence grows when children are given the tools necessary to live on their own rather than taught to be dependent upon someone else as the toolholder.

My children have been choosing their own clothes since they were very small. I would offer them a choice of two outfits: "Do you want to wear this or that?" I reinforce their good color pattern selections and suggest an alternative if patterns or colors clash. I heard very early, "I do it myself!"

— ❧ —

Whenever possible, give your child the choice. What to have for breakfast. What to wear. Who to invite over to play. Which book to read. What chore to do. The point is not to open the world wide without limits but rather to give your child limited options, all of which you are comfortable with, and then offer within these limits the complete freedom to choose.

Allow for the Experience of Natural Consequences

Nagging is telling a child over and over and over again something he already knows. Independence is offered when a child is encouraged to listen internally to what he knows he should be doing, and then to follow through on his own or endure the natural consequences that follow.

The trick here? Don't rescue! Don't play Helicopter Mom, hovering overhead and then swooping down to help the minute our children stumble. When we rescue, we rob children of the opportunity to learn perseverance. We give them the misperception that life will be fair and fun and that if it isn't, Mom will be there to fix it. Such a Fix It Mom actually becomes an enabler, who takes over the child's responsibilities and consequences, and subtly teaches the child that he cannot live effectively on his own.[16]

We find it difficult to stand back and not interfere in our children's lifestyles. Why? We have more wisdom, of course!

— ❧ —

Let your children make mistakes and experience what happens when they do. Follow the advice of family psychologist John Rosemond, who cautions, "The more parents try to make their children happy, the more they prevent their children from learning how to make themselves happy."[17]

Refuse to Do for Them What They Can Do for Themselves

When you leave a responsibility, action, or attitude on your child's shoulders rather than taking it over, you allow them to grow.

Ask yourself, "Is this my problem or my child's?" A lost shoe is her problem. When you start owning the responsibility of looking for the shoe, she quits. Help your child understand that it is her problem. Of course you care about her problem and sometimes you even help her with her struggles, but you will not take her problem from her and make it yours. (Now, if your child can't find her shoe, and you have to be somewhere in ten minutes, part of the problem may become yours and you would help her! Or tell her she must wear different shoes, which becomes part of the consequence of not keeping track of her shoes.)

I remember teaching two of my children how to ride a bike, running beside them and hearing them constantly plead, "Don't let go, don't leave me." All the while, I had already let go. They just needed to know I was still beside them.

— ❧ —

GETTING TO THE HEART
OF LET-ME-GROW-UP LOVE

"The purpose of raising a child, simply stated," says family psychologist John Rosemond, "is to help that child get out of your life and into a successful life of his or her own. If that sounds a bit cold, it's only because we tend to think sentimentally, rather than practically, about the raising of children. It has nothing to do with rushing the child out of the family as quickly as possible. It simply means that it's the job of parents to slowly but surely help the child stand alone in every way—socially, emotionally, and financially. This is, after all, every child's mission."[18]

Our children need Let-Me-Grow-Up Love. They need a combination of nurturing and nudging. They need to be given responsibilities so they can learn to respond. By trying and failing and learning and succeeding. When we meet that need and see them growing into people who need us less, we know that we are doing our job.

Love Handles

LOVE HANDLE #1:

General Guidelines for Nurturing Independence

- Recognize that your child is separate from you. Respect his or her individuality.
- Letting go is a process that demands a gradual change in the way a parent demonstrates love from infancy— through total control and responsibility—to maturity— through no control and no responsibility.

- The process is marked by an orderly transfer of responsibility and control as the child grows up. Each year, intentionally increase the child's freedom. Celebrate the milestones of independence.
- The process has two goals: it weans the child from the parent; and weans the parents from the child.
- Recognize your goals. You raise your children to leave you. Parenting is a temporary job description.
- Seek balance in your life as your child grows up. Don't depend upon his or her successes to be your successes. Encourage them to pursue their own dreams, not your expectations.[19]

LOVE HANDLE #2:

Boundaries and Consequences

Respect for boundaries helps a child move toward independence. These guidelines might help a parent establish boundaries.

1. Consequences are intended to increase the child's sense of responsibility and control over his life. A system of rewards and consequences should not build a sense of helplessness, but help a child make choices for his own benefit. Dragging a child into his room to make him clean is less effective than establishing a system so that he chooses to clean it.
2. Consequences must be age-appropriate.
3. Consequences must be related to the seriousness of the infraction.
4. The goal of boundaries is an internal sense of motivation, with self-induced consequences. Successful parenting means that our kids want to get out of bed and

go to school, be responsible and caring because that's important to them, not because it's important to us.[20]

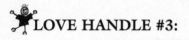

LOVE HANDLE #3:

Positive Steps to Self-Discipline

Here are some steps to becoming a more disciplined person, whether a child or an adult.

1. Learn to face frustration. Things will not always turn out the way you want.
2. Learn to deal with boredom. The only way to overcome boredom is to face boring tasks and to complete them as quickly as possible.
3. Learn to identify fears—and deal with them. Fear of failure and fear of criticism are two big obstacles.
4. Stop rationalizing your procrastination. Immediate activity keeps you from falling into the cesspool of good intentions, which are never followed through.
5. Learn self-denial. Getting things done usually means giving up something else.
6. Learn to deal with feelings of inferiority. These emotions have to be replaced with notions of security and self-sufficiency.
7. Learn to deal with periods of disenchantment. Highs and lows are a natural part of life.[21]

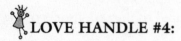

LOVE HANDLE #4:

Messages of Responsibility

Here are some basic messages we try to pass on to our children to help them build a sense of responsibility and self-discipline:

- I am responsible for my own happiness.
- I am responsible for my own possessions.
- I am responsible for my own time.
- I am responsible for my own success.
- I am responsible for my own health.
- I am responsible for my own habits.
- I am responsible for my own attitude.[22]

 **LOVE HANDLE #5:**

Kindergarten Readiness

Q: Our daughter is five. How long in advance should we start preparing her for kindergarten?

A: You have already started to prepare your daughter. How you've talked about children carrying their lunch boxes, what you've said about your own school experiences, and how you approached kindergarten registration have already helped her shape her opinion of school.

More targeted preparation begins about a month before school opens, perhaps around the same time ads for school supplies fall out of the Sunday newspaper. This will be a good time to include your daughter in buying decisions regarding a backpack, new shoes, and anything else included on the supply list mailed from your school. Listen carefully as your daughter shares her feelings about schedule changes and new friends.

Avoid the pitfall of making kindergarten your only topic. School should be one item on the agenda, but not the only one. Continue to support your child's play times with neighborhood friends and her out-of-school activities. Some children need a greater sense of continuity than others, but all students need reassurance that familiar parts of life will continue, even though there is a major change coming.[23]

LOVE HANDLE #6:

Before a Child Leaves Home . . .

Consider the qualities or skills you want your child to acquire in order to be self-sufficient before leaving home at about age eighteen. Making a list of those skills helps you aim toward tangible goals. These skills are not learned in the last few weeks before a child leaves home, so each year you intentionally move toward these goals with age-appropriate steps.

- Personal Care:
    Brush and floss teeth
    Shampoo and style hair
    Clean and cut nails
    Bathe
    Make dental and doctor appointments
- Clothing Maintenance:
    Sort, wash, and fold laundry
    Iron
    Shop wisely
    Mend clothes and sew on buttons
    Polish shoes
    Hem pants and skirts
- Food Preparation:
    Plan balanced meals
    Shop wisely
    Cook and bake
    Follow recipes
    Set table
    Wash dishes
    Store food properly
- House Maintenance:
    Change and make beds
    Dust, vacuum

Clean mirrors and windows
Sweep, mop floors
Care for plants
Separate items for recycling[24]

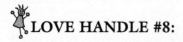

LOVE HANDLE #7:

Questions for Moms

1. What goals of independence do you have for your child?
   - by kindergarten
   - by third grade
   - by sixth grade
2. Will you nurture your child's need for independence in the same way or differently from the way your parents raised you?
3. What are the ways you are tempted to overprotect or "hold on" to your children? Why?
4. Define your child's unique personality. If you have more than one child, define their differences and how you will raise them differently based on these differences.
5. What privileges and responsibilities are you giving your child this year over last year?
6. How are you maintaining a balance at home between your children's needs and your needs?
7. How are you changing the way you show your love to your child as he or she grows up?

LOVE HANDLE #8:

"Letting Go Is . . ."

To let go doesn't mean to stop caring, it means I can't do it for someone else.

To let go is not to enable, but to allow learning from natural consequences.

To let go is to admit powerlessness, which means the outcome is not in my hands.

To let go is not to care for, but to care about.

To let go is not to fix, but to be supportive.

To let go is not to be in the middle arranging all the outcomes, but to allow others to effect their own outcomes.

To let go is not to be protective; it is to permit another to face reality.

To let go is not to deny, but to accept.

To let go is not to nag, scold, or argue, but to search out my own shortcomings and to correct them.

To let go is to fear less and love more.

Anonymous

MOM READING:

Children Who Do Too Little, Patricia Sprinkle
Developing Your Child's Temperament, Beverly LaHaye
Give Them Wings, Carol Kuykendall
Learning to Let Go, Carol Kuykendall
Loving, Launching, and Letting Go, Virelle Kidder
The Measure of Our Success, Marian Wright Edelman

LAP READING:

Best Friends Sleep Over, Jacqueline Rogers
Don't Forget to Write, Martina Selway
Ira Sleeps Over, Bernard Waber
When Will I Read? Miriam Cohen
Will I Have a Friend? Miriam Cohen

Nine

Hope:

Help-Me-Hope Love

"But Mommy, what will I do every day without Meagan? Nothing will be any fun!" five-year-old Ashley asked. Her eyes filled with tears as she and her mother looked out the window across the street at Meagan's house. Both knew that tomorrow the movers would come and pack up Meagan's home and take Meagan and her family far away to live in another state.

Debbie had dreaded this day. Meagan and Ashley had been "best friends" for over two years. Ever since they'd been old enough to actually enjoy a friend, they'd chosen each other. Mornings in Meagan's sandbox, tea parties in Ashley's bedroom, summer afternoons splashing in the plastic pool, evenings on the swing set. Behind her brave maternal facade, she too wondered how her daughter would manage without her kindred spirit friend.

But Debbie was prepared. Weeks ago, she determined that on this day, she would let the house go, hang her baby on her hip, and make Ashley happy by giving the two girls a bang-up good-bye celebration. She'd already cleared the twenty-four-hour final fun-a-thon with Meagan's mom. So she planned a sleep over, a movie, and make your own ice-cream sundaes.

"Meagan will be here in a just a minute, and we're going to have such a great time!" The doorbell rang, and Ashley

217

whirled to answer it. Debbie was right. From that moment until late that night when the two girls fell asleep tucked into the same bed, they had *fun*!

The next morning came, and with it, the moving van. At breakfast they were poking fingers through the holes in doughnuts making "rings" when they suddenly looked at each other and said, "This is the day!" Meagan raced to the front windows with Ashley shadowing a few steps behind. They gazed at the huge yellow truck parked across the street. Its wide ramp spread out toward the sidewalk like a tongue gobbling up every piece of furniture from Meagan's house.

Immediately, Debbie distracted them. "Okay girls, time for a bubble bath! Bring your dolls, and you can all take one together!" Slowly Meagan and Ashley followed her to the bathroom. She kept it up all morning long. Around noon, she tucked the girls into the car to get them out and away from the spectacle across the street and headed to the park. A picnic on the jungle gym. Leftovers fed to the ducks. Chunks of chalk for sidewalk drawing. Bubble-blowing. As many pushes on the swings as they wanted.

Returning in the late afternoon, they drove up their street to find the moving truck just closing its doors, and Meagan's family loading the last of their personal items in their van. It was time. Meagan sprang from the car, excited now at the adventure of the move. Ashley followed her, hesitating. They hugged. Meagan scampered toward her own family. Everyone waved. Doors slammed. The giant yellow truck started up and chugged off, followed by Meagan's family's van, with Meagan waving silently from the back window. A ceiling of clouds now covered the late afternoon sky.

Debbie turned to instigate "Stage Three" of her plan with Ashley. "Okay, Sweetie, it's time for ice cream—before dinner! We're going to have a great time—you and me and the baby!"

But Ashley stood like a statue, unresponsive to her mother's enthusiasm. She stared down the street at the spot where Meagan's van had vanished.

"My tummy is too sad for ice cream."

Debbie understood her daughter's feelings, but she wanted to fix her sadness. "What is it you need, Ashley?" she asked. "I'm willing to try anything." Behind Ashley she could see some sunbeams streaming from the clouds that surrounded the setting sun. They peeked out from behind the clouds like reminders that the sun was still there. Sunbeams promising sunshine. Promising a better tomorrow. A brighter future. Another day.

"Hope. That's what you need, Ash, isn't it? You need to know you'll see Meagan again sometime. And that you'll find another friend to play with soon."

Her words must have touched something in Ashley because now she buried her face against her mother's jeans and cried. Standing in the driveway, Debbie looked at the dark windows of Meagan's house and wrapped her arms about her young daughter.

THE MEANING OF HOPE

Trying to define and give hope can be as difficult as trying to capture a sunbeam and handing it to your child. And yet, life without hope is unimaginable and—more to the point—unlivable. We must have hope in life.

Pastor and Dallas Seminary President Chuck Swindoll believes hope is basic to life: "Hope . . . is something as important to us as water is to a fish, as vital as electricity is to a light bulb, as essential as air is to a jumbo jet."[1]

How true are his words! In a storm, hope is believing the wind will cease and the rain will stop. In the darkness of night, hope is knowing morning will come again. When we've fallen,

My children have a need for hope. This is a need with eternal consequences.

— ❧ —

hope is the promise that we can get back up. Hope is faith that "the sun will come out tomorrow" as Little Orphan Annie belted out. Hope is knowing there is more to life than just this moment, that there is something yet to come. Hope is believing in potential: flowers waiting to bud, discoveries still to be made, and explorations to enjoy.

Children need Help-Me-Hope Love. Life will not always shield them in loving protection. Life is hard. And hope provides the resilience needed to live it well.

Born to Hope

Naturally, intrinsically, children are born to hope. They come from the womb with the fight for life and the perseverance to continue.

When I get on my boys too much my oldest reminds me, "I'm a gift from God, Mommy." That always calms me down and puts things back into focus. Ask your children to remind you they're gifts—it makes them feel good too!

— ❧ —

An Italian adage says, "God and the child speak the same language." Indeed! Almost beyond logic, children believe the best about people. They grant forgiveness readily and with ease. They give and receive love with gusto. They are optimistic. It is their nature. They know nothing else and so rapidly rise to offer hope even in dark places.

When Hope Bumps into Life

But, like all of us, children eventually discover that life isn't fair. They grow confused when the innocence of hope bumps into the hard rock reality of life's disappointments, such as death, divorce, loss, separation, brokenness, transition, and sickness. These obstacles sadly stop a child and rob him of hope.

In these moments, when childlike optimism meets hard rock reality, children need the gift of Help-Me-Hope Love, a kind of love that reaches past what is confusing and brings the restoration of calm.

THE GIFT OF HOPE

This gift of hope is two-fold. It holds both a present comfort and a future promise.

A Present Comfort

Hope provides a present comfort for life. Like a trusted, favorite blanket, it wraps a child in the assurance that all is well. When you kiss an owie and "make it better" you give Help-Me-Hope Love. When you wipe away the tears after a friend has been cruel, you give Help-Me-Hope Love. When you whip up a favorite meal after an absence, bundle up a sick child on pillows before the TV, or offer open arms to hug a disappointed child, you provide Help-Me-Hope Love.

There is a comfort in hope that eases pain and soothes sorrow. *This moment will pass. You are not alone in life. Someone loves you and will stay by your side when you are hurting.*

A Promise for Tomorrow

Hope also gives a promise for tomorrow. It shines, like a night-light in a dark nursery, with the dependable truth that darkness will not win. A sense of perspective in hope promises another day, another feeling, another chance. It leads young lives forward past mistakes, through pain, and beyond the disappointment to what is next in life.

My seven-year-old drew a picture of a scraggly bush among giant trees. She said, "Mom, the trees are the other kids in my class, and the bush is me." So I took the picture and turned the bush into a beautiful rosebush full of roses, and colored it in. When she saw the picture, she put it up on her bulletin board as a reminder that she is valuable and loved for herself and that she is precious to God.

— ❧ —

When you remind a child of her uniqueness after an older kid has ridiculed her, you give Help-Me-Hope Love. When you say prayers together, tuck him in, and kiss him good night, you focus his gaze on tomorrow and all that it can bring. You help him let go of today. You help him believe . . . *Sorrow is something you go through, not something you end with. Pain is part of life, but not all of life. Every day won't feel like this sad day feels.*

MOM AS A HOPE-BRINGER

When a child's hope is hurt, that child often looks wide-eyed to mom to provide renewal. And as moms, we dig down deep in our own hearts, rummaging about for what we might offer. We want so much to come through for our little ones!

How to Bring Hope

Usually, we can find several treasures to hold out as hope.

Bring understanding

Every one of us has days when "unwonderful" things happen. Sometimes they're our own fault. And other times, they simply occur, through no one's fault. Hope comes when someone else seems to understand, without fixing or judging.

In her book *When a Hug Won't Fix the Hurt*, Karen Dockery says that to heal, you must "accept your child's feelings and your feelings. Denying feelings or holding them in causes a festering wound. As you accept, express, and respond to feelings, you and your child will find healing and wholeness."[2]

Sit down with your child and ask him about his feelings. Then listen, without editing or evaluating. Repeat back what you hear him saying. Put yourself inside your child's feelings and share a time when you were in a similar spot. The gesture of understanding gives your child the hope he needs.

Bring wonder

Children naturally enjoy the wonder of life. But when they've been wounded or disappointed, they may lose their sense of wonder. In such moments, we can bring wonder back by reflecting it to them.

Lie down on the grass on your tummies and search for ladybugs. Catch one and let it crawl across your palm. Notice its trust when it doesn't even know who is holding it. Take a stroll and stop to watch ants build hills in the sidewalk cracks. Share your awe at their creativity and perseverance, when in a flash, their home could be ruined by rain or a person who steps on it.

In the everyday moments of life, wonder sparkles and provides hope. Bring wonder by magnifying such marvels for your child.

Bring joy

Even the most painful moment can be a hiding place for joy or contentment. This doesn't mean being a sappy, always-happy kind of person. Rather, when we learn to find something to enjoy, even in the midst of the unpleasant, we bring hope. In the trip to the doctor's office for an allergy shot, we help the child look forward to feeling better tomorrow. In the rainy day that alters the birthday party plans for a trip to the zoo, we let the child choose the movie to show and the game to play as a replacement.

Choose to start the day in a good mood because your mood is contagious to others around you, and they might find themselves feeling optimistic in response. Lighten up. Laugh. At yourself. At your mistakes. At odd occurrences. At inconveniences and interruptions. Be content with what you have rather than always wishing for more than you have. Point out the good. Dark colors give pictures depth and dimension. Bees may sting, but they also multiply flowers. Rain interrupts a picnic, but it also makes the grass green.

When you find joy and contentment in glum circumstances, you bring a vital ingredient of hope.

Bring gratefulness

No matter how dreary a day may feel, someone somewhere is experiencing a day yet more dreary. An attitude of gratitude breeds hope.

Play an "I'm thankful for ..." game at mealtime. Have each person share something to be grateful for before each bite. Pull out a family picture album and sit together remembering "good times." Invest time and energy in serving someone else who has needs. Children's rights advocate Marian Wright Edelman reminds us that " ... service is the rent we pay for living. It is the very purpose of life and not something you do in your spare time."[3] When we focus our attention on the needs of others, we are made freshly aware of our own good fortune. This too breeds hope.

As moms, we have a unique opportunity to be Hope-Bringers for our children. Who knows them as we do? Who cares for their future as we do? Who believes they deserve the best, can be the best, and are the best as we do? Bring hope? "Oh yes!" we say, "That's what I want to bring my child!"

Bumps to Bringing Hope

Understanding. Wonder. Joy. Gratefulness. Oh how much we want to provide this Help-Me-Hope love for that child we love so dearly! But at times we look for where to get these things to offer, and we come up empty ourselves. We bump into our own needs.

> *When I make a mistake, I try to say so. I want my children to know that I am not perfect either.*
>
> — ❧ —

"I don't know how to bring hope."

Sometimes we bump into confusion or inadequacy as to how to bring hope to our child. Maybe his feelings of sadness or anger are so strong that they actually scare us. Maybe we aren't sure if our child needs hope or needs counseling. "I don't know how to do this. I need help. Where is the specialist?" we wonder.

"I have no hope."

In many moments, we find ourselves struggling without hope. How can I bring my child hope when I have none? The daddy that left my little girl was my husband. The mother of my daughter's friend who moved away was my best friend. The sickness my child faces means the death of my dreams for her.

When our child bumps into obstacles in life, we stiffen with paralysis. We can't help. When we ourselves have no hope, we cannot give our child hope.

"I want to be my child's hope."

And then some of us moms believe deep inside that it is our job to be our child's hope. We're Fix It Moms who intervene every time our child has a struggle. We redo the school project late at night. We try to patch up the friendship after our child has a fight with a buddy. We make moving day an extravaganza to disguise the pain.

But even when we've given our best efforts, stepped into spot after spot to protect our child and provide hope, we eventually come face to face with the reality that we simply aren't enough. Someday life will hand them—and therefore us—a circumstance we can't fix . . . a death, a divorce, a disease, a disappointment. What then?

LASTING HOPE

In such moments, our child needs more hope than we can offer. And we realize, finally, that we cannot meet this need for hope by ourselves.

Lasting Hope for You, Mom

It comes down to this: no mom is enough to meet all her child's needs. You can't do it. It's impossible. The needs of your child for security, affirmation, family, discipline, guidance, respect, fun, independence, and . . . hope . . . are more than *any* mother can provide in and of herself. You can *help* meet these needs. You can go a long way toward meeting them. But you, Mom, cannot entirely meet your child's needs all by yourself.

You know that, don't you? You get tired and grouchy. You make mistakes. Your needs bump into the needs of your child.

Here's the truth: your child needs more than you. The moment you understand that statement may be the most important moment of motherhood for you. More than anything in the world, you want to be there for your child. You want to meet her needs in a meaningful way. When you realize that you can't be enough for your child, you face what you lack: your own need. You need hope beyond yourself. And you can find it.

It's been said that "God offers us eternal hope, something that goes beyond what the world has to offer."[4] That's what you need, Mom. There's not enough of you to meet all the needs of your child. But there is enough of God. And when you ask him to meet your needs, he can help you help your child.

God wants to help you by bringing you into a relationship with him. You see, hope comes in a relationship. Through a relationship with God's son, Jesus, your needs can be met completely and permanently. You can begin this relationship right now just by praying a simple prayer, "Dear Jesus, I know that I am not enough and that I cannot be enough by myself. I have holes and inadequacies in who I am. I need you. Please come into my life."

Then, decide to nurture this relationship each day through reading the Bible, through prayer, and through getting involved in a community of others who need God: the church.

Theologian Karl Barth was once asked what was the most profound truth he had ever heard. He quickly replied, "Jesus loves me, this I know. . . ." Along similar lines, spiritual leader and author James Bryan Smith wrote, "What we long to know is that we are loved . . . we hunger to know that we are accepted as we are, forgiven for all we have done, and cared for by a gracious, loving God. . . . When we know this, we walk away well. When we know this, we have hope."[5]

Hope comes when we realize our own need for it and learn to meet it in God. Wendy C. Brewer, a mother, says it so well in her poem below.

Today I didn't say the right things
I didn't give enough hugs
I didn't listen to all of their imaginary stories.
Today I hurried them through what could have been
very special moments, to achieve my binding agenda.
Today my prayers were too short and
my lectures too long.
My smiles, I'm sure, didn't hide my fatigue.
Today I didn't heal any wounds;
in fact, I'm sure I caused some.

Their tears fell and I felt too lifeless
to wipe them away.
Today I felt completely defeated and totally inadequate
for this position called "mommy."
But as I kneel in prayer to confess my failures, I am re-
      minded . . .
I am not their hope.
I am not their joy.
I am not their salvation.
He is!
And they are his children even more than they are mine.
I am reminded . . .
he always listens,
always guides,
always touches,
and always loves perfectly.
I can rest now, Lord, remembering
that I am not alone.[6]

Mom, when we have lasting hope, we are in a secure and
strong position to give the Help-Me-Hope Love our child so
desperately needs.

Lasting Hope for Your Child

When a child experiences love through Mom, she receives
her first glimpse of God's love. In giving Hold-Me-Close Love,
Crazy-About-Me Love, and Let-Me-Grow-Up Love, among
others, we meet our children's needs. But because our love is
imperfect and inconsistent, we need to help our child come to
know God's love, which is perfect and consistent.

Sofia Cavalletti, author of *The Religious Potential of the
Child*, writes, "I think there is a very deep correspondence between the child and God, because both are very rich in love.

The child is very capable of receiving love, but also of giving love. And most of the time, I think children are disappointed with adults because we have our limits. . . . I think the best mother and best father have their limits, after all. With God the children really have found the right partner for them."[7]

As moms, we are uniquely equipped to be hope-bringers to our children. And when we understand our own need for lasting hope in a relationship with God, we are able to bring this final and most vital ingredient of hope to our children: faith.

Part of my job as a mom is to help prepare the soil—to loosen it, hopefully, with an atmosphere that says, "God is good," to feed it with Bible stories, prayer, and nurturing people, and to pull some of the weeds such as unfavorable influences or maybe too many activities. God plants the seed and provides the sunlight and rain.

— ❧ —

Bring hope through a relationship

Children love to hear about God. They are naturally interested in the Bible and in the stories of Jesus' miracles and power. When they come to understand their own imperfections, that they will disobey even though they mean to obey, that they will choose selfishly or that they feel awful feelings even toward those they love, they also come to understand their need for God to help them.

Very simply, explain to your children how much Jesus loves them. Talk to them honestly about your own mistakes and how God loves you enough to forgive you. Then help your children ask Jesus for help. Jesus wants very much to have a relationship with your children from the time they are tiny. They do not have to go through life alone, wondering whether there is hope. Jesus is their hope, just as he is your hope.

Bring hope through prayer

Teach your child to pray. You can do this by example—just praying together over meals or stopping to pray specially at naptime or bedtime. You can also do this by using little prayers that you read together from a child's prayer book. Or you can invite your child to pray himself. Simple prayers uttered in moments of need and in moments of delight underline the fact that a relationship with God is just that: a relationship. He wants to hear our hurts and our concerns. He listens carefully because he loves us.

Bring hope through community

Involve your children with you in church. Church can be a wonderful partner with you in building hope through faith. Sunday school teachers can teach Bible stories and lessons. Children can learn about the needs of people in other parts of the world through World Missions and those in your own city through service programs.

GETTING TO THE HEART OF GIVE-ME-HOPE LOVE

Think back to the pain little Ashley experienced when her friend Meagan moved away. We understand clearly that what Ashley needed was a sunbeam of hope, a reminder that there was a present comfort and a future promise. Debbie couldn't provide this hope by merely "fixing" Ashley's day with ice cream or fun activities. But she could give her daughter hope by gently leading her to Jesus, who is the Comforter and Promise for all our days.

You see, we won't always be there, Mom. Our children will grow up and away to live on their own. In the process, we want to point them toward the One who will give them all that they need for a full and meaningful life. And they will need:

Security: Hold-Me-Close Love convinces them they are unconditionally loved.

Affirmation: Crazy-About-Me Love underlines that they are cherished.

Family: Fit-Me-Into-the-Family Love communicates their significance and sense of belonging.

Discipline: Give-Me-Limits Love provides the protection of boundaries for life.

Guidance: Show-Me-and-Tell-Me Love gives them what they need to know in life.

Respect: Let-Me-Be-Me Love accepts them for who they are.

Play: Play-With-Me Love allows them to do the work of play.

Independence: Let-Me-Grow-Up Love offers permission and freedom to mature.

Hope: Help-Me-Hope Love conveys an eternal perspective, that there is more to life than just today.

We can meet these needs in part. We can get up each morning intending to make a difference in the life of a child that will equip her for a bright future. But in the end, all we can do is our best, and then we must surrender the responsibility for that life to that child. And to God.

Hope is the ultimate offering of love. It points a child in the direction of help outside of herself. It offers a tool that can be sharpened independently for use day in and day out through her life no matter where she ends up.

Hattie Vose Hall penned a poem that portrays a mother's unique manner of being a Hope-Bringer to her child.

A personal relationship with God is vital to making parenting successful.

— 🐾 —

A builder built a temple, he wrought it with care and skill—
Pillars and groins and arches, all fashioned to do his will.
And men said as they saw its beauty, "It shall never know
    decay."
Great is thy skill, O Builder! Thy fame shall endure for
    years."

A mother built a temple, with infinite love and care,
Planning each arch with patience, laying each stone with
    prayer.
None praised her unceasing efforts, none knew of her won-
    drous plan.
for the temple the mother built was unseen by the eye of
    man.

Gone is the builder's temple—crumpled into the dust;
Low lies each stately pillar, food for consuming rust.
But the temple the mother built will last while the ages roll.
For that beautiful unseen temple was a child's immortal
    soul.[8]

Love Handles

 **LOVE HANDLE #1:**

Dealing with a Mom's Challenges About Hope

(A variation of 1 Corinthians 13)

Though I lecture and harp at my children and have
not love, I will be background noise to rebellious thoughts.
    And though I wisely warn them not to use the street
as a playground, or they'll be killed; and though I patiently

explain why snails live in mobile homes, and I give endless answers to life's other mysteries, and though I have faith that can remove mountains of ignorance—yet never hug my children—I have taught nothing.

And though I slave over a steaming stove with balanced diets and complicated recipes and even burn my fingers—yet never smile as I serve—I have not really fed them.

A truly loving mother suffers through unfinished sentences, clutter, nicks on furniture, sleepless nights, and adolescent insults, and is kind enough to think her kids are the greatest. A loving mother tries not to resent her children for being free like she used to be, and doesn't brag about how she never talked to her mom that way.

Real love: considers a childish nightmare more urgent than her need for sleep; is not shattered by the title "Meanest Mom"; and does not smirk as her child trips over the toy he refused to put away (but with silent wisdom rejoices in the effective lessons of experience).

Mother-love has strong arms from lifting, a heart large with believing, a mind stretched with hoping, shoulders soft with enduring, and knees bent with committing.

True mother-love never fails to point her child to the Author of Love.[9]

LOVE HANDLE #2:

How to Help Your Child Know God

When you meet your child's need for hope through knowing God, you give your child:

- A sense of security. Children feel safer knowing that a loving Creator is looking after them. Religious rituals and traditions also give children a sense of security.
- A sense of justice. Children encounter cruelty and injustice early on. Knowing that good will ultimately be

rewarded and evil punished can help a child persevere in rough times.

Here are some age-appropriate ways to meet that need for hope through knowing God:

- Birth to Three:
  Let your toddler hear you pray or sing hymns.

  Teach your child to pray at meals or bedtime.

  When she asks questions—"Who made the flower?"—be simple and direct with your answer: "God did." Help your child see God in creation.

- Three to Five:
  Answer their questions. They will ask questions like, "What does God wear? Where does God live?" Try turning the question around and asking the child: "What do you think God wears?"

  Use hands-on learning because they learn by doing. Seek church classes that use hands-on learning.

  Read children's Bible stories out loud.

  Let your child see your faith. Talk to him about God.[10]

LOVE HANDLE #3:

Hearing God's Promises

Choose some of God's short, simple promises and begin to plant them like seeds in your child's heart. When children are young, they memorize easily and those promises will come back to comfort them for the rest of their lives. Here are a few:

"The LORD watches over you . . ." Psalm 121:5

"The LORD will keep you from all harm . . ." Psalm 121:7

"I the LORD do not change . . ." Malachi 3:6

"Love comes from God . . ." 1 John 4:7

"Come to me, all you who are weary . . . and I will give you rest . . ." Matthew 11:28

"I am with you always . . ." Matthew 28:20

"I can do everything through him who gives me strength . . ." Philippians 4:13

"We know that in all things God works for the good of those who love him . . ." Romans 8:28

"For nothing is impossible with God . . ." Luke 1:37

"The joy of the LORD is your strength . . ." Nehemiah 8:10

"You will pray to him, and he will hear you . . ." Job 22:27

LOVE HANDLE #4:

Building Hope Through Happy Attitudes

We know that attitudes are contagious. As moms, we set the tone and build our children's hopefulness or hopelessness through our attitudes and responses. Here is a H.A.P.P.Y. acrostic to remind us:

H appiness is a choice.

A ccept pain as sad. Bad things happen, and it's okay to feel sad. But the sadness won't last forever.

P repare. Store blessings up in your heart. Discover God's provision in everyday miracles, like the smiles of your children and the sun that comes up daily without fail.

P ersist in bringing out the good. Cooperation, encouraging words, honesty, and understanding are the glue that hold our lives together.

Y our children will teach you. As you guide your children through difficult or painful times, learn from them. Young children have a natural optimism, spontaneous love, a bent toward hope. Nurture and encourage that.[11]

LOVE HANDLE #5:

Helping Children Understand Death

Children need to find hope as they begin to comprehend the meaning of death. Here are descriptions of a child's view of death, and suggested ways to respond:

- Birth to 3 Years
  At this age, children become more upset by change than death; change directly affects them. A child may cry, throw tantrums, or misbehave because a parent coping with death is upset and may be inadvertently neglecting the child.

  Ways to Respond: Maintain routine. Provide a loving atmosphere. Hug the child. Hold him or her on your lap. Reassure child that you won't leave him.

- 4 and 5 years
  Preschoolers tend to think death is reversible. They believe a dead person or animal will wake up. One four-year-old thought that sprinkling water on a dead kitten would bring the animal to life. Another child thought his grandfather had gone on a "long trip" and would return.

  Ways to Respond: Don't use euphemisms. A child who hears a dead person has "gone away" or "gone to sleep" will literally think the person will come back. Explain that the dead person's body wore out or stopped working, not just that he or she was sick. Otherwise, children may fear they'll die the next time they catch a cold. Assure them that they aren't at risk.[12]

LOVE HANDLE #6:

Family Prayers

Evangelist Billy Graham lists reasons why having family prayers is important:

1. It unifies the home life and puts faith in the place of friction.
2. It brings to the family group a sense of God's presence.
3. It shows the children that God is relevant to everyday living and not just a Being to be worshiped at church.
4. It gives members of the family an opportunity for self-examination and confession of sin.
5. It strengthens the members of the household for the tasks and the responsibilities they are to face during the day.
6. It insulates us against the hurts and misunderstandings that come our way.
7. It supplements the work of the church and makes our homes a sanctuary where Christ is honored.[13]

LOVE HANDLE #7:

Praying with Children

Help children use their own words to talk to Jesus in prayer. Here are some sentence starters that they can finish in their prayers.

Jesus, I think you are wonderful because . . .

The story I like best about You is . . .

The one way I would like to be more like You is . . .

Please help me today to . . .

I want to be nicer to . . .

I know you were with me today because . . .[14]

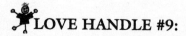LOVE HANDLE #8:

The Family "God Hunt"

A "God Hunt" means looking for God's touch on our everyday world and is based on the children's game of "Hide and Seek." It builds upon that exhilarating feeling that children had when waiting for a companion to give a clue that would reveal himself. This is a spiritual game played in the same way, seeking, keeping your eyes and ears open to God's presence. When you find him, you can shout, "I spy!" which means you have found God at work in your life. Four suggested clues will get you started on your family "God Hunt." Look for God in:

1. Answers to prayers.
2. Any unexpected evidence of God's care.
3. Any unusual linkage or timing.
4. Any help to do God's work in the world.[15]

LOVE HANDLE #9:

Successful Family Devotions

Gathering together as a family for prayer and Bible reading sounds wonderful, but young children often get bored and restless. Here are three suggestions:

1. Keep them short: Think about your children's ages and how long they can reasonably sit still. Five minutes may be as long as they can listen.

2. Keep them happy: Happy family devotions grow out of happy family relationships. Check on your "happy" quotient. Examine your family life and determine to work on family relationships that are bumpy or grumpy. Try singing grace together or a song and talk about the words.

3. Keep them varied: Keeping family worship happy also means keeping it varied. For instance:
   - Let different family members lead.
   - Act out a Bible story.
   - Take a nature walk and collect things that God has made.
   - Talk about what is going on in the world, the community, in the life of each family member.
   - Talk about the ways to show God's love to others in the family or neighborhood. Write them on slips of paper and put them in a jar or box. Take them out during the week and do them. Ideas include keeping the living room clean, pulling weeds, writing a thank-you note, or drawing a picture for someone.[16]

MOM READING:

1001 Ways to Introduce Your Child to God, Kathie Reimer
31 Days of Praise, Ruth Myer
Answers to Tough Questions, Josh McDowell and Don Stewart
Eerdmans' Book of Famous Prayers, compiled by Veronica Zundel
Embracing the Love of God, James Bryan Smith
Faith Training: Raising Kids Who Love the Lord, Joe White
Hope Again, Charles R. Swindoll

Mom's Devotional Bible (NIV Version)
Your Child's Faith, Dr. Larry Stephens
Teaching Your Child About God, Wes Haystead

LAP READING:

The Bible in Pictures for Little Eyes, Kenneth Taylor
Gospel Light Family Prayer Calendar, Shirley Dobson and Pat Verbal
Grandma, I'll Miss You, Kathryn Slattery
Heart to Heart Bible Stories, Amy Grant
Little Visits for Toddlers, Mary Manz Simon
The Rag Coat, Lauren Mills
Read-Aloud Bible Stories, Ella K. Lindvall
The Rhyme Bible, Linda Sattgast
Someday Heaven, Larry Libby
Tell Me the Story, Max Lucado
Wee Sing Bible Songs, Pamela C. Beall and Susan H. Nipp
Wise Words for Little People, Kenneth Taylor

The MOPS Story

MOPS stands for Mothers of Preschoolers, a program designed for mothers with children under school age. MOPS meets the needs of every mom—urban and suburban moms, stay-at-home and working moms, teen, single, married moms—moms with different lifestyles who all share a similar desire to be the very best moms they can be!

MOPS encourages moms through resources, such as books, the MOPS International Web site, and MOMSense radio and magazine. MOPS also helps moms through relationships, established in the context of MOPS groups that provide a caring atmosphere for today's mothers of young children. In a MOPS group, a mom has an opportunity to share concerns, explore areas of creativity, and hear instruction from a MOPS Mentor that equips her for the responsibilities of family and community. The MOPS group also includes MOPPETS, a loving, learning experience for children.

MOPS began in 1973 when a small group of moms met in a local church near Denver to share their common needs. Today, approximately 2700 groups meet in churches throughout the United States, Canada, and 17 other countries, reaching 100,000 women and their families. Mothers of preschoolers lead MOPS groups, so they have the chance to develop their leadership skills through experience and excellent training opportunities.

Find out how MOPS International can help you become part of the MOPS*to*Mom Connection.

MOPS International
P.O. Box 102200
Denver, CO 80250-2200
Phone 1-800-929-1287 or 303-733-5353
E-mail: Info@MOPS.org
Web site: http://www.MOPS.org

To learn how to start a MOPS group,
call 1-888-910-MOPS.
For MOPS products call The MOPShop
1-888-545-4040

Notes

Introduction

1. Angela Thole, "A Mother's Prayer," Riverside MOPS, Bloomington, MN, 1996.

Chapter One

Security: Hold-Me-Close Love

1. Urie Bronfenbrenner, "Discovering What Families Do," David Blankenhorn, Steven Bayme, Jean Bethke Elshtain, editors, *Rebuilding the Nest: A New Commitment to the American Family* (Milwaukee, WI: Family Service America, 1990), 31.

2. John Bowlby, *Attachment*, Vol. 1 of *Attachment and Loss* (New York: Basic Books, 1969), 77.

3. Sharon Begley, "Your Child's Brain," *Newsweek* (February 19, 1996): 55–61.

4. John Bowlby, *Separation: Anxiety and Anger*, Vol. 2 of *Attachment and Loss* (New York: Basic Books, 1973), 204.

5. Sigmund Freud, *Outline of Psychoanalysis*, 2nd ed. (London: Hogarth Press, 1940), 188.

6. Dr. Henry Cloud and Dr. John Townsend, *The Mom Factor* (Grand Rapids: Zondervan, 1996), 13. Used by permission of Zondervan Publishing House.

7. Brenda Hunter, *In the Company of Women* (Sisters, OR: Multnomah Books, 1994), 49.

8. Deborah Shaw Lewis and Charmaine Crouse Yoest, *Mother in the Middle* (Grand Rapids: Zondervan, 1996), 92–93.

9. Katherine Butler Hathaway, *The Journal and Letters of the Little Locksmith* (New York: Arno Press, 1980).

10. Cloud and Townsend, 25.

11. Ron Hutchcraft, *5 Needs Your Child Must Have Met at Home* (Grand Rapids: Zondervan, 1994), 88–89. Used by permission of Zondervan Publishing House.

12. William Damon, *Social and Personality Development* (New York: W.W. Norton and Company, 1983), 87. As quoted in Brenda Hunter, Ph.D., *In the Company of Women* (Sisters, OR: Multnomah Books, 1994), 34.

13. Foster Cline, M.D., "Understanding and Treating the Severely Disturbed Child," (Evergreen, CO: Evergreen Consultants in Human Behavior.)

14. Cloud and Townsend, 61.

15. John Drescher, *Seven Things Children Need* (Scottdale, PA: Herald Press, 1976), 44–45.

16. William Coleman, *If I Could Raise My Kids Again* (Minneapolis, MN: Bethany House Publishers, 1996), 122.

17. Lowell Ponte, "The Sense that Shapes our Future," *Readers Digest* (January 1992): 21–24.

18. Gary Smalley, *The Key to Your Child's Heart* (Waco, TX: Word Books, 1984), 75.

19. Ross Campbell, M.D., *How to Really Love Your Child* (Wheaton, IL: Victor Books, 1977), 40.

20. Mary Manz Simon, *Front Porch Parenting* (Colorado Springs, CO: Chariot Victor Publishing, 1997), 42.

21. Ruth Bell Graham, source unknown.

22. Valerie Bell, *Getting Out of Your Kids' Faces and Into Their Hearts* (Grand Rapids: Zondervan, 1994), 31. Used by permission of Zondervan Publishing House.

23. Adapted from Elisa Morgan and Carol Kuykendall, *What Every Mom Needs* (Grand Rapids: Zondervan, 1995), 133–34.

24. Adapted from Ron Hutchcraft, *5 Needs Your Child Must Have Met at Home* (Grand Rapids: Zondervan, 1994), 81–82. Used by permission of Zondervan Publishing House.

25. Coleman, 123.

Chapter Two

Affirmation: Crazy-About-Me Love

1. Dr. Henry Cloud and Dr. John Townsend, *The Mom Factor* (Grand Rapids: Zondervan, 1996), 27. Used by permission of Zondervan Publishing House.

2. Ross Campbell, M.D., *How to Really Love Your Child* (Wheaton, IL: Victor Books, 1977), 35.

3. Campbell, 57.

4. Susan L. Lenzkes, *When the Handwriting on the Wall is in Brown Crayon* (England: CWR Publishers, 1997), 92. Used with permission.

5. Thomas Lickona, "Raising Good Children," *The Denver Post* (January 22, 1984): 10.

6. John Drescher, *Seven Things Children Need* (Scottdale, PA: Herald Press, 1976), 77.

7. *Mommy I Love You Just Because . . .*, MOPS International (Grand Rapids: Zondervan, 1997).

8. Gary Smalley, *The Key to Your Child's Heart* (Waco, TX: Word, 1984), 67.

9. Leola Floren, *The New Boss has a Milk Mustache* (Kansas City, MO: Beacon Hill Press, 1996), 14.

10. Clyde Narramore, "Ten Ways You Can Shape a Child's Life," (Narramore Christian Foundation, 1975).

11. Adapted from *Today's Christian Woman* (July–August 1990): 60.

12. Adapted from Valerie Bell, *Getting Out of Your Kids' Faces and Into Their Hearts* (Grand Rapids: Zondervan, 1994), 133–34. Used by permission of Zondervan Publishing House.

Chapter Three

Belonging: Fit-Me-Into-the-Family Love

1. Dr. Henry Cloud and Dr. John Townsend, *The Mom Factor* (Grand Rapids: Zondervan, 1996), 26. Used by permission of Zondervan Publishing House.

2. John Drescher, *If I Were Starting My Family Again* (Intercourse, PA: Good Books, 1994), 45.

3. John Drescher, *Seven Things Children Need* (Scottdale, PA: Herald Press, 1976), 43.

4. Blair Justice, Ph.D., "The Ties That Heal," *Better Homes and Gardens* (November 1989): 48.

5. Marian Wright Edelman, *The Measure of Our Success* (Boston, MA: Beacon Press, 1992), 75.

6. Drescher, *Seven Things Children Need,* 74.

7. Janis Long Harris, *What Good Parents Have in Common* (Grand Rapids: Zondervan, 1994), 125.

8. Dr. James Dobson, "Focus on the Family" tape series (Waco, TX: Word, 1978).

9. Delores Curran, *Traits of a Healthy Family* (Minneapolis, MN: Winston Press, 1983), 217–18.

10. Foster W. Cline, M.D. and Benjamin W. Brucker, Ed.D., *Success in Parenting* (Spokane, WA: Lon Gibby Productions, Inc., 1996), 6.

11. Cindy Sumner, "Growing with Grandparents," *MomSense* (Spring 1996): 5.

12. Cindy Sumner, "Toys at Grandma's House," *MomSense* (Spring 1996): 5.

13. Karen Dockrey, *Growing a Family Where People Really Like Each Other* (Minneapolis, MN: Bethany House, 1996), 80–81. Used with permission. Available from your local bookstore or call 1-800-328-6109.

14. Elisa Morgan, "Your Family's Coat of Arms," *Mom's Devotional Bible* (Grand Rapids: Zondervan, 1997), 766.

Chapter Four

Discipline: Give-Me-Limits Love

1. Ron Hutchcraft, *5 Needs Your Child Must Have Met at Home* (Grand Rapids: Zondervan, 1994), 135. Used by permission of Zondervan Publishing House.

2. Dr. Henry Cloud and Dr. John Townsend, *Boundaries* (Grand Rapids: Zondervan, 1992), 41. Used by permission of Zondervan Publishing House.

3. Randolph K. Sanders, *A Parent's Bedside Companion* (Scottdale, PA: Herald Press, 1992), 97.

4. Claudia Arp, *PEP Groups for Moms: Building Positive Relationships with Your Children* (Elgin, IL: David C. Cook, 1994), 46.

5. Ross Campbell, M.D., *How to Really Love Your Child* (Wheaton, IL: Victor Books, 1977), 88.

6. Dr. Henry Cloud and Dr. John Townsend, *The Mom Factor* (Grand Rapids: Zondervan, 1996), 94. Used by permission of Zondervan Publishing House.

7. Erma Bombeck, *Forever Erma* (Kansas City, KS: Andrews and McMeel, 1996), 42–43.

8. Cloud and Townsend, *The Mom Factor*, 94.

9. Hutchcraft, 135.

10. Dr. Grace Ketterman, *Mothering* (Elgin, IL: Christian Parenting Books, David C. Cook, 1991), 286.

11. Foster W. Cline, M.D. and Benjamin W. Brucker, Ed.D., *Success in Parenting* (Spokane, WA: Lon Gibby Productions, Inc., 1996), 36.

12. Ketterman, 266.

13. Cline and Brucker, 60.

14. Adapted from Cloud and Townsend, *Boundaries*, 185–88. Used by permission of Zondervan Publishing House.

15. Cline and Brucker, 57.

16. Dr. James Dobson, *The Strong-Willed Child* (Wheaton, IL: Tyndale House, 1984), 31–33.

17. Adapted from Ketterman, 283–84.

18. Adapted from Arp, *PEP Groups for Moms* (Elgin, IL: David C. Cook, 1994), 48.

19. Adapted from Dr. Mary Manz Simon, *Front Porch Parenting* (Colorado Springs, CO: Chariot Victor Publishing, 1997), 50–51.

20. Adapted from John Rosemond, "Turning Mixed Signals To Straight Talk," *Better Homes and Gardens* (June 1986): 96.

21. Cline and Brucker, 41.

22. Adapted from William and Nancie Carmichael, *Lord, Bless My Child* (Wheaton, IL: Tyndale House, 1995), 30.

23. Dr. James Dobson, *The New Dare to Discipline* (Wheaton, IL: Tyndale House, 1990), 245.

Chapter Five

Guidance: Show-Me-and-Tell-Me Love

1. Elisa Morgan, *Mom to Mom* (Grand Rapids: Zondervan, 1996), 67.

2. Gary Smalley, *The Key to Your Child's Heart* (Waco, TX: Word Books, 1984), 136–55.

3. Gloria Gather, "What I Would Give My Children," *Sunday Digest* (March–May 1995, Section 11, May 14): 2–3.

4. Sue Lockwood Summers, *Media Alert! 200 Activities to Create Media-Savvy Kids* (Castle Rock, CO: Hi Willow Research and Publishing, 1997), VI.

5. John Rosemond, "Parents Get Inaccurate Info About ADD," *The Sunday Camera* (July 7, 1996): 2F.

6. Permission to use granted by Ann Landers and Creator's Syndicate.

7. Dr. Henry Cloud and Dr. John Townsend, *The Mom Factor* (Grand Rapids: Zondervan, 1996), 62. Used by permission of Zondervan Publishing House.

8. Cloud and Townsend, 63.

9. Melicint Margaret Trimble, "Someone's Following Us," source unknown.

10. Sybil C. Waldrop, *Guiding Your Child Toward God* (Nashville, TN: Broadman Press, 1985), page unknown.

11. John Drescher, *If I Were Starting My Family Again* (Intercourse, PA: Good Books, 1994), 16.

12. Marian Wright Edelman, *The Measure of Our Success* (Boston, MA: Beacon Press, 1992), 35–78.

13. Lyle E. Bourne Jr. and Bruce R. Ekstrand, *Psychology: Its Principles and Meanings* (New York: Holt, Rinehart and Winston, 1976), 305–24.

14. Pat Hershey Owen, *The Idea Book for Mothers* (Wheaton, IL: Tyndale House, 1981), 60–61.

15. Summers, *Media Alert!*, viii.

16. Sue Lockwood Summers, "Media Literacy: Training Tips for the Home," (Littleton, CO: *Prime Time Today*, 1994).

17. Summers, *Media Alert!*, 1.

Chapter Six
Respect: Let-Me-Be-Me Love

1. Charles R. Swindoll, *You and Your Child* (Nashville, TN: Thomas Nelson, 1977), 21.

2. Cynthia Ulrich Tobias, *The Way They Learn* (Colorado Springs, CO: Focus on the Family, 1994), 147.

3. Randolph Sanders, *A Parent's Bedside Companion* (Scottdale, PA: Herald Press, 1992), 23.

4. John Drescher, *If I Were Starting My Family Again* (Intercourse, PA: Good Books, 1994), 18.

5. Christopher de Vinck, *Simple Wonders* (Grand Rapids: Zondervan, 1995), 111.

6. Kima Jude, "Gifts Every Mother Wants," *Virtue* (May–June 1996): 44.

7. John Powell, S.J., *Unconditional Love* (Allen, TX: Argus Communications, 1978), 66–68.

8. Ron Hutchcraft, *5 Needs Your Child Must Have Met at Home* (Grand Rapids: Zondervan, 1994), 24. Used by permission of Zondervan Publishing House.

9. Gary Smalley, *The Key to Your Child's Heart* (Waco, TX: Word Books, 1984), 27–34.

10. Ken Gire, *Windows of the Soul* (Grand Rapids: Zondervan, 1996), 18.

11. Charles Stanley, "Let Your Kids Know You Care," *Moody* (November 1986): 88.

12. Kelly A. Kim, "Cleaning Up," *Welcome Home* (October 1996): 7. Reprinted with permission of the author.

13. Valerie Bell, *Getting Out of Your Kids Faces and Into Their Hearts* (Grand Rapids: Zondervan, 1994), 104–7. Used by permission of Zondervan Publishing House.

14. John K. Rosemond, "Respecting Your Child," *Hemispheres* (February 1995): 99.

15. Excerpted and adapted from Cynthia Ulrich Tobias, *Every Child Can Succeed* (Colorado Springs, CO: Focus on the Family, 1996) 20–21, 72.

16. Dr. Henry Cloud and Dr. John Townsend, *Boundaries* (Grand Rapids: Zondervan, 1992), 50. Used by permission of Zondervan Publishing House.

Chapter Seven
Play: Play-With-Me Love

1. Miriam Huffman Rockness, *A Time to Play* (Grand Rapids: Zondervan, 1983), 77.

2. Evelyn Bence, "Growing Creative Kids," *Today's Christian Woman* (July–August 1985): 78.

3. Marlene LeFever, "Homegrown Creativity," *Moody* (March 1984): 72.

4. William Coleman, *If I Could Raise My Kids Again* (Minneapolis, MN: Bethany House, 1996), 121.

5. David Elkind, *The Hurried Child* (Reading, MA: Addison-Wesley, 1981), 9.

6. Dr. Grace Ketterman, *Mothering* (Elgin, IL: Christian Parenting Books, David C. Cook, 1991), 294.

7. Leslie Rhea Seifert, "Thank You, God, for Children," *MomSense* (Winter 1996): 4.

8. Judy Ford, *Wonderful Ways to Love a Child* (Berkeley, CA: Conari Press, 1995), 99.

9. Terry W. Glaspey, "Recapturing the Wonder," *Inklings* (Spring 1996): 7.

10. Patricia H. Sprinkle, *A Gift From God: Meditations for New Mothers* (Grand Rapids: Zondervan, 1994), 54.

11. Liz Curtis Higgs, *Only Angels Can Wing It* (Nashville, TN: Thomas Nelson, 1995), 76–77.

12. William and Nancie Carmichael, *Lord, Bless My Child* (Wheaton, IL: Tyndale House, 1995), 132.

13. Carole Wright, "My Mom Took Us Out in the Rain," Phoenix, AZ, 1994.

14. Walt Wangerin Jr., *Little Lamb, Who Made Thee?* (Grand Rapids: Zondervan, 1993), 19–20. Used by permission of Zondervan Publishing House.

15. Karen Dockrey, *Growing a Family Where People Really Like Each Other* (Minneapolis, MN: Bethany House, 1996), 47. Used by permission. Available from your local bookstore or call 1-800-328-6109.

16. Rockness, 77.

17. Tom Eisenman, *Temptations Families Face* (Downers Grove, IL: InterVarsity Press, 1996), 176.

18. Elizabeth Fenwick, *101 Essential Tips for Baby Care* (New York: DK Publishing, 1996), inside cover.

19. Adapted from Jennifer L. Goran, "Let Them Play," *Focus on the Family* (March 1994): 14.

20. Adapted from Karen Dockrey, *Growing a Family Where People Really Like Each Other* (Minneapolis, MN: Bethany House, 1996), 151–52. Used by permission. Available from your local bookstore or call 1-800-328-6109.

21. Dockrey, 154–56.

Chapter Eight

Independence: Let-Me-Grow-Up Love

1. Dr. Henry Cloud and Dr. John Townsend, *Boundaries* (Grand Rapids: Zondervan, 1992), 66. Used by permission of Zondervan Publishing House.

2. Carol Kuykendall, *Learning to Let Go* (Grand Rapids: Zondervan, 1985), 10.

3. William and Nancie Carmichael, *Lord, Bless My Child* (Wheaton, IL: Tyndale House, 1995), 36.

4. Carmichael, 36.

5. Elisa Morgan, *Mom to Mom* (Grand Rapids: Zondervan, 1996), 81.

6. Randolph K. Sanders, *A Parent's Bedside Companion* (Scottdale, PA: Herald Press, 1992), 98.

7. Joan Merrill, taken from a MOPS group newsletter.

8. Cloud and Townsend, *Boundaries*, 186.

9. Ruth Bell Graham, *Prodigals and Those Who Love Them* (Colorado Springs, CO: Focus on the Family, 1991), 44.

10. Susan L. Lenzkes, *When the Handwriting on the Wall is in Brown Crayon* (England: CWR Publishers, 1997), 24. Used by permission.

11. A.W. Tozer, *The Pursuit of God* (Harrisburg, PA: Christian Publications, Inc., 1976), 28.

12. Carol Kuykendall, *A Mother's Footprints of Faith* (Grand Rapids: Zondervan, 1997), 87.

13. Dr. Henry Cloud and Dr. John Townsend, *The Mom Factor* (Grand Rapids: Zondervan, 1996), 91. Used by permission of Zondervan Publishing House.

14. Ron Hutchcraft, *5 Needs Your Child Must Have Met at Home* (Grand Rapids: Zondervan, 1994), 141. Used by permission of Zondervan Publishing House.

15. Hutchcraft, 143.

16. Cloud and Townsend, *The Mom Factor*, 94.

17. John Rosemond, "Your Best is Always Good Enough and Other Musings on Parenthood," *Boulder Daily Camera* (February 13, 1994).

18. John Rosemond, "Raising an Independent Child," *Better Homes and Gardens* (November 1990): 42.

19. Adapted from Carol Kuykendall, *Learning to Let Go* (Grand Rapids: Zondervan, 1985), 21.

20. Adapted from Cloud and Townsend, *Boundaries*, 191–92.

21. Adapted from Earl D. Wilson, *Self Discipline* (Portland, OR: Multnomah Press, 1983), 11–20.

22. William Coleman, *If I Could Raise My Kids Again* (Minneapolis: Bethany House, 1996), 103.

23. Adapted from Dr. Mary Manz Simon, *Front Porch Parenting* (Colorado Springs, CO: Chariot Victor Publishing, 1997), 55–56.

24. Adapted from Patricia Sprinkle, *Do I Have To?* (Grand Rapids: Zondervan, 1993), 77.

Chapter Nine

Hope: Help-Me-Hope Love

1. Charles R. Swindoll, *Hope Again* (Dallas, TX: Word Publishing, 1996), 3.

2. Karen Dockery, *When a Hug Won't Fix the Hurt* (Wheaton, IL: Victor Books, 1993), 27.

3. Marian Wright Edelman, *The Measure of Our Success* (Boston, MA: Beacon Press, 1992), 6.

4. Eugene Peterson, *The Message of Hope* (Colorado Springs, CO: NavPress, 1994), 3.

5. James Bryan Smith, *Embracing the Love of God* (San Francisco, CA: Harper, 1995), 3.

6. Wendy C. Brewer, "Today . . ." Printed in *Decision* (May 1996): 39. Published by the Billy Graham Evangelistic Association.

7. Sofia Cavalletti, "Teaching us the Source of Joy," *Sojourners* (January 1987): 23.

8. Adapted from Hattie Vose Hall, *The Messenger* (Vail Bible Church, Pastor Rich Teeters June, 1995).

9. Susan L. Lenzkes, *When the Handwriting on the Wall is in Brown Crayon* (Grand Rapids: Zondervan, 1982), 19.

10. Adapted from Anne Cassidy, "Teaching Kids About God," *Working Mother* (December 1995): 36–43.

11. Dockery, 166–69.

12. Jolene L. Roehlkepartain, "Age Level Insights: Death," *Children's Ministry* (Redeemer Presbyterian Church, Winston-Salem, NC).

13. Billy Graham, *My Answer* (Garden City, NY: Doubleday Co, 1960), 56.

14. Adapted from Chapel of the Air, "Prayer—An Adventure with God," *Evangelizing Today's Child* (November/December 1987): 22.

15. Adapted from Karen and David Mains, "The Family God Hunt," (Carol Stream, IL: Chapel of the Air, Inc., 1993).

16. Bruce and Mary Shelley, "Keeping Boredom from Preying on Family Praying," *Focal Point*, Vol. 5, No. 3 (July-September 1985).

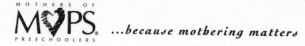

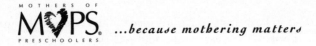

Make Room for Daddy
A Mom's Guide to Letting Dad Be Dad

ELISA MORGAN AND CAROL KUYKENDALL

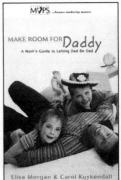

In most families, new moms spend a lot of time thinking about their role as mothers and how to meet the needs of their young children. But most of the books on raising children are geared to mothers; not much has been written about the important role Daddy plays in the day-to-day care of a young child and how Mom influences that role. *Make Room for Daddy*, by seasoned MOPS International authors Elisa Morgan and Carol Kuykendall, is uniquely addressed to moms to help them understand these principles:

*Children need dads as well as moms.
*Moms and dads are different. A dad will love and parent his children differently from mom. These differences are good, and children need both kinds of love as they grow up.
*Men tend to want to be good dads, just as women want to be good moms.
*Moms influence their children's fathers in powerful ways by making room for Daddy.

Elisa and Carol base their advice on careful research and the results of questionnaires to more than a thousand moms and dads, and they both share personal reflections, revealing their own struggles to let their husbands be dads in their unique ways.

The book is divided into three parts: "A New Style," about the "birth of a father" into his new role; "Mommy Style"; and "Daddy Style." There is also a "What to Do Next" section, page after page of how-to's or practical applications of the principles of this book.

At the end of each chapter is a Make Room for Reflection section with questions appropriate for small group or personal reflection. Each chapter also concludes with Top Tips about Pops from MOPS—helpful suggestions from MOPS moms.

Softcover ISBN 0-310-24044-1

Pick up a copy today at your favorite bookstore!

GRAND RAPIDS, MICHIGAN 49530

WWW.ZONDERVAN.COM

We want to hear from you. Please send your comments about this book to us in care of the address below. Thank you.

ZONDERVAN™

GRAND RAPIDS, MICHIGAN 49530

WWW.ZONDERVAN.COM